D1078598

Canary
Islands

Berlitz

Canary Islands

Original text:	Norman Renouf
Updater:	Pam Barrett
Editor:	Media Content Marketing, Inc
Photography:	Chris Coe except page 24 by Roger Williams and page 38 by Nigel Tisdall
Cover Photograph:	Richard Passmore, gettyimages
Photo Editor:	Naomi Zinn
Layout:	Media Content Marketing, Inc.
Cartography:	Ortelius Design
Managing Editor:	Tony Halliday

Ninth Edition 2003
Updated 2005

CONTACTING THE EDITORS

Every effort has been made to provide accurate information in this publication, but changes are inevitable. The publisher cannot be responsible for any resulting loss, inconvenience or injury. We would appreciate it if readers would call our attention to any errors or outdated information by contacting Berlitz Publishing, PO Box 7910, London SE1 1WE, England. Fax: (44) 20 7403 0290; e-mail: berlitz@apaguide.co.uk; www.berlitzpublishing.com

Printed in Singapore by Insight Print Services (Pte) Ltd, 38 Joo Koon Road, Singapore 628990. Tel: (65) 6865-1600. Fax: (65) 6861-6438

Berlitz Trademark Reg. U.S. Patent Office and other countries. Marca Registrada. Used under licence from the Berlitz Investment Corporation

CONTENTS

• A ▶ in the text denotes a highly recommended sight

Canary Islands

THE ISLANDS AND
THE PEOPLE

More than 1,000km (620 miles) south of the Iberian Peninsula and just 115km (70 miles) from the nearest point on the African coast, an archipelago made up of 13 volcanic islands juts dramatically out of the Atlantic Ocean. These, the Canary Islands, are an integral part of Spain, although they now have their own island government, known as the Cabildo Insular. Six of the islands, Alegranza, La Graciosa, Lobos, Montaña Clara, Roque del Este and Roque del Oeste, are no more than specks in the sea and remain uninhabited. Of the others, it is the eastern islands, the three closest to Africa – Gran Canaria, Lanzarote and Fuerteventura – that are geologically the oldest, and as they have the most extensive coastal shelf, they also have the most beaches.

The four western islands, Tenerife, La Palma, La Gomera and El Hierro, in descending order of size, have ragged coastlines with cliffs rising vertiginously out of the ocean. Of these, however, only Tenerife has beaches of any size, and the golden sands that make them so popular have usually been imported from the Sahara or rescued from the bottom of the sea. In total, the archipelago has approximately 1,500km (930 miles) of coast and the characteristic, intensely blue waters are due to the ocean's depth – as much as 3,000m (9,840ft) between some of the islands.

Geographically within the bounds of the Tropic of Cancer, the surrounding ocean is somewhat cooler than would be expected at such a sub-tropical latitude. The Gulf current arrives from the north and the ensuing trade winds that brush the islands brings the Canaries, at sea level at least, an extremely genial climate. Average temperatures on the beaches vary around 19°C (66°F) in winter and 25°C

(77°F) in summer. However, many of the islands are mountainous – Mount Teide on Tenerife rises to 3,718m (12,195ft) and not only dominates the archipelago but is the highest mountain in Spain. Such altitudes means that the temperatures can vary dramatically, not only between islands, but within islands as well.

The combination of such a climate and the unusual geological features have given rise to an amazing array of flora and fauna, which thrives even though none of the islands has a running river. The isolation of the archipelago has also played its part in the preservation of these natural gifts. In fact, with around 650 native plant species, it is one of the most important areas in the world, comparable only with other archipelagos such as Hawaii and the Galapagos. Recognising this, and intent upon preserving it, the Law of Natural Areas in the Canaries has created nature and rural parks, nature reserves, nature monuments, protected landscapes and areas of scientific interest, with the intention of limiting human activity in the zones. These amount to no less than 36 percent of the archipelago's territory.

But what about the people of the Canary Islands? Governed by the Spanish since the end of the 15th century the Canarians, to outsiders, look Spanish, speak Spanish, are imbued with Spanish culture and to all intents and purposes are little different – except perhaps that they are somewhat quieter and less volatile in character than their mainland cousins. However, throughout the centuries the Canary Islands have acted as a bridge between Europe, Africa and the Americas and as a consequence have become home to numerous people originating from disparate cultures, especially from the Latin American countries that were once Spanish colonies. The result, today, is a people who regard themselves as Canarian first and Spanish second.

Capturing the king – playing chess in the Parque de Santa Catalina, Las Palmas, is taken very seriously.

The islanders learned, in the second half of the 20th century, to capitalise on their natural resources – the fine climate and splendid beaches that attract so many visitors from northern Europe and other places. It may come as a surprise, especially given the former Soviet Union's serious economic problems, that many of the brochures advertising tourist attractions now include descriptions in Russian. Tourism is a massive business. The most recent figures available from the Department of Tourism and Transport show that around 10 million people per annum visit the Canaries. Of these, close to 4 million head for Tenerife, 3½ million to Gran Canaria and just over 1 million each to Lanzarote and Fuerteventura, while La Palma attracts only about 100,000. Certain areas, mainly the southern coasts of Gran Canaria and Tenerife, and to a lesser but growing extent Lanzarote and Fuerteventura, cater to mass tourism, while the smaller islands, that lack commercially exploitable beaches, will always lag well behind in numbers, if not in their natural attractions. It would seem that with so many visitors, the islands would be perpetually crowded, but this is not so, as most people head directly for the major resorts, such as Playa de las Américas on Tenerife and Playa del Inglés on Gran Canaria. In fact, if all the land devoted to tourism were to be added up, it would still occupy only a mere fraction of the islands' total area and natural wealth.

So which is the best island for you? It may be a cliché, but it is nonetheless true, that there is something for everyone. The diversity of landscapes on the islands is quite amazing. Snow capped mountains, beautiful, verdant valleys, deserts, towering cliffs and wonderful beaches of golden or black sand can all be found in the Canaries and some islands have intriguing combinations of these characteristics. Remember, the Canaries are volcanic, and volcanic islands are never dull. Teneguia, on La Palma, erupted as recently as 1971. On Lanzarote you can not only gaze at the awesome scenery created by

Parts of the volcanic landscape are splashed with vivid green in spring.

earth-shattering events that occurred centuries ago, you can also watch your lunch cooking over the heat of the volcano beneath your feet *(see page 141)*.

Tenerife is the biggest island and has plenty to show for it. Mount Teide offers the grandest scenery and the island certainly has the greatest number of tourist attractions by day and night. In terms of all-round appeal, however, Gran Canaria runs a close second. Both islands have bustling modern cities and sleepy old towns to visit; both have dramatic and strikingly beautiful interiors; and both have busy resorts ranging from raucous to tranquil.

If a long stretch of golden beach is a priority, then southern Gran Canaria has the edge. Lanzarote, with its stark *malpaís* (badlands), will delight those who are environmentally aware yet enjoy the company of other visitors. Whether or not the continued growth of tourism there erodes this delicate balance remains to be seen, but the tourist attractions masterminded by local artist César Manrique (1919–92) combine well with those of resorts like Puerto del Carmen, and the general ambience of this island, with its low-rise, whitewashed buildings is extremely appealing.

Fuerteventura tends to polarise opinion: it is truly a desert island – wind-swept, sandy and barren. Is it an oasis in the middle of an over-complicated world, as some have claimed, or simply the desert that it seems at first glance? The beaches here are certainly the best in the Canaries and resorts to suit most tastes are springing up. Aside from watersports, for which it has a high reputation, there isn't a great deal to do or see. The lesser known and much smaller islands of La Palma, La Gomera and El Hierro do not have that many beaches and have therefore escaped mass tourism and should continue to do so, although they are cultivating low-key *turismo rural*. The lack of commercial attractions this brings has, in these three islands, become an attraction in itself. There are relatively few hotels and restaurants of note (although enough for discerning visitors), no discos and blaring bars to disturb the peace and best of all – as far as many are concerned – very few tourists. There is a bountiful supply of beautiful mountainous scenery and, if you search hard enough, a pleasant beach or two to relax on. If this is your idea of a dream holiday, one of these quieter islands may be perfect for you. For most people, though, a day or two away from it all is enough. Island hopping is easy and a few days on an unspoiled island combined with the creature comforts of a major resort offer the best of both worlds. Travel independently, look out for the unexpected, and you will soon discover that the Canary Islands have much more to offer than just an all-year suntan.

Santa Cruz de Tenerife, joint capital of the Canary Islands, is a modern city yet retains an island charm.

A BRIEF HISTORY

The Canary Islands are a place of myths and legends. Many writers link the lost continent of Atlantis with the Canaries. According to Plato this rich, happy land, somewhere west of Gibraltar in the Atlantic Ocean, was destroyed by earthquakes and tidal waves nearly 12,000 years ago. After the cataclysm only the mountain tops of Atlantis remained above the sea and constituted seven islands. Could this have been the Canaries? The ancient Greeks thought of the islands as the Garden of Hesperides, and the Romans called this archipelago the 'Insulae Fortunatae', the Fortunate Islands.

The author Plutarch wrote of fertile lands somewhere off the coast of Africa, where the breezes of springtime never stop. His source was the Roman leader Sertorius, who had heard of the lands from an explorer. In the 1st century AD Pliny wrote of an expedition to the islands by King Jube II of Mauretania, who apparently saw many dogs roaming the islands. *Canis* is the Latin for dogs, hence Canary Islands.

From Plato to Jules Verne the possibilities have stirred people's imagination, ranging from academic theories to eccentric ramblings. The truth is lost in the mists of time, but what is undeniable is the magical presence of these seven volcanic islands. When you sight Mount Teide on a distant horizon you will understand the profusion of legends.

The First Inhabitants

Long before the first European sailors arrived, all seven Canary Islands were inhabited. The original people are known as Guanches, meaning 'man' in the native tongue. Strictly speaking, this name applies only to the inhabitants of Tenerife, but has come to be widely used for the indigenous people of the whole archipelago.

The Castillo de San José on Lanzarote bears witness to the repeated attacks on the Canary Islands.

The Guanches are thought to have arrived in the islands around the 1st or 2nd century BC, probably from North Africa. Ethnographers link them with the Cro-Magnon and Proto-Mediterranean race. They were tall, light-skinned, often blue-eyed and fair-haired. You can see their remains in the meticulous collection of the Museo Canario in Las Palmas on Gran Canaria *(see page 56)*. Here too you can study their preoccupation with death. Like the ancient Egyptians they carefully embalmed their dead, presumably for a ceremonial passage to the next world. Cryptic rock carvings have been found that may explain these rituals, but so far no one has found the Canarian version of the Rosetta Stone with which to decipher them.

Another mystery is how these early people arrived on the islands, as no evidence of Guanche boats has ever been discovered. One theory is that they may have floated across from North Africa on craft made of reeds. The expeditions of Thor Heyerdahl lend some credence to this idea and the concept is explored in great detail at the Pyramids of Güímar on Tenerife *(see page 34).*

The Guanches were cave dwellers, although many of the caves that remain today were probably used only for storage.The Cenobio de Valerón near Gáldar on Gran Canaria, for example, although called a convent, was probably only a grain store. Cave dwelling in such a climate is a logical idea, being cooler in summer and warmer in winter than more conventional accommodation. Even today, there are many cave dwellings in the islands.

A Guanche legacy that you will see at the market place and in traditional eating houses is *gofio*, a finely-ground, toasted flour that is still a traditional Canarian staple. The Guanche language also lives on in such place names as Tafira and Tamadaba (on Gran Canaria), Timanfaya (on Lanzarote), Teide (on Tenerife) and Tenerife itself.

Conquistadors

The first foreign visitors to the Canaries are thought to have been Arab sailors who landed on Gran Canaria some 2,000 years ago and were met warmly. In later centuries the islanders' gracious hospitality was to cost them dearly.

Europeans did not arrive until the 14th century, when the Genoese sailor Lanzarotto Marcello colonised the island, known then in the native language as Tytheroygatra and subsequently as Lanzarote. Slave traders, treasure seekers and missionaries all followed in Lanzarotto's wake, but it was not until 1402 that the European conquest of the Canaries began in earnest. At its helm was the Norman baron, Jean de Béthencourt, in the service of Henry III of Castile. After the baron had taken Lanzarote and Fuerteventura with comparative ease, his ships were scattered by storms off Gran Canaria. He next turned to El Hierro, where the awestruck islanders welcomed as gods the new visitors arriving in their great floating vessels. Béthencourt returned the hospitality by inviting the natives aboard his ships. He then took them captive and sold them into slavery.

Around this time the Portuguese, who had also been colonising the Atlantic, turned their attention to the Canaries. Naval skirmishes ensued between the two powers, but at the end of the war of succession between Portugal and Castile, the wide-ranging Treaty of Alcaçovas ended Lisbon's claims to the Fortunate Islands.

By order of Ferdinand and Isabella of Castile, the second phase of the conquest was set in motion. By 1483 Gran Canaria had been subdued and in 1488 Gomera was taken. La Palma held out until 1493 and after another two years of furious fighting, the biggest prize of all, Tenerife, was in Spanish hands. The process of pacification and conversion to the Christian faith had taken almost a century of bloody guerilla warfare with thousands of casualties, sustained mainly on the brave but ill-equipped Guanche side.

Discovering the New World

Just as the conquest of the Canaries was reaching its climax, Christopher Columbus (Cristóbal Colón in Spanish) was planning his expedition in search of a sea route to the East Indies. Each of the Canaries claims some connection with Columbus, who came to the islands because they were then the world's most westerly charted points and therefore the last stopping point before venturing into the unknown.

The great navigator stopped off at La Gomera and at Las Palmas (for ship repairs) on his voyage of 1492 and he recorded a volcanic eruption while passing Tenerife. His crew took this as an ill omen but, as history tells us, once past El Hierro they did not drop off the edge of the world after all. Columbus's routes and Canarian connections may be traced at the atmospheric Casa de Colón in Las Palmas *(see page 56).*

The role of the islands as a bridge between the Old World and the New has continued through the centuries. Canarians have settled in Latin America in large num-

A bust of Columbus looks out over Vegueta in Las Palmas de Gran Canaria.

bers, usually in search of a better way of life, and news from Venezuela and Cuba is treated almost as a local item in the Canary Islands newspapers. Canarian bananas provided the stock for those of the Carribbean and in accent and musical rhythms the speech of the Canaries lie halfway between Spain and South America.

Wine and Warfare

The Canaries' first major agricultural enterprise was sugar. Sugar cane sprouted easily on the islands and during the first half of the 16th century a burgeoning industry developed.

Boom turned to bust, however, with cheaper sugar production from Brazil and the Antilles, and the industry died.

Still, trade links had at least been established with both the Old and the New Worlds, and wine became the new venture to bolster the economy, especially in Tenerife. Grapes grown in the volcanic soil produced a distinctive, full-bodied malmsey wine *(malvasía)* that became the fashionable drink of aristocratic Europe. Shakespeare and Voltaire, among others, were lavish in their praise and today's island visitors can still sample the excellent wine in *bodegas*, restaurants, or even from the *supermercado*. When touring the islands you may still see old disused wine presses *(lagares)* on hillsides.

By the end of the 18th century the Canaries were a sufficiently important trading point to attract all types of incursions. In 1797, Admiral Horatio Nelson attacked

Agriculture is still an important part of the economy, although competing in the international market is tough.

Santa Cruz de Tenerife in search of a Spanish treasure ship. The defenders responded vigorously, accounting for the lives of 226 British sailors and the removal of the lower part of Nelson's saluting arm. The Santa Cruzeros clearly had no hard feelings towards Admiral Nelson, however. Once it was known that the attack had been repelled, a gift of wine was sent out to his ship (England was, after all, an important wine market) and a street was later named Calle de Horacio Nelson, in his honour.

Free Trade

By the early 18th century Canarians had become fully Spanish in both outlook and loyalties and many volunteers fought in the Peninsular War (Spaniards call it the War of Independence), which ended in 1814 with the restoration of Ferdinand VII to the Spanish throne.

Economic problems arose in the early 19th century and the wine industry started to fail. Luckily another single-crop opportunity presented itself in the form of cochineal, a parasitic beetle attracted to the *opuntia* variety of cactus. The tiny bodies of the female bugs contain a dark-red liquid perfect for dyeing and for 50 years or so, millions of bugs were crushed for the sake of the Canarian economic good.

The bubble burst with the rise of chemical dyes in the 1870s. With the failure of yet another monoculture, the Spanish government felt constrained to help the Canarian economy. In the mid-19th century, free-port status was granted by royal decree to one port in each of the islands (two in Tenerife). The lowering of duties and trade barriers at a time of considerable shipping expansion had the desired effect and Santa Cruz de Tenerife and Las Palmas soon became two of the world's busiest ports. British entrepreneurs also invested a lot of money in the port of Las Palmas.

The most recent monoculture was bananas. The first exports were made in the 1880s, but the trade's runaway success did not outlast World War I. However, the cultivation of the small, sweet bananas continued to be a mainstay of the islands' economy for as long as mainland Spain was able to provide a guaranteed market.

In 1912, Cabildos (Island Councils) were created and given the responsibility for the social, political and economic administration of each island and coordination with the Ayuntamientos (Town Halls). This led, in 1927, to the Canaries being divided into two provinces; Santa Cruz de Tenerife with the western islands of Tenerife, La Palma, La Gomera and El Hierro; and Las Palmas de Gran Canaria with the eastern islands of Lanzarote and Fuerteventura.

The Spanish Civil War

The plot that sparked off the Spanish Civil War was hatched in the Canary Islands. In 1936 a group of senior officers, discontented with the policies of the Spanish Republican Government, met in secret in the woods of La Esperanza on Tenerife. They had come to meet a fellow officer, Francisco Franco, a right-wing nationalist whom the government had packed off to the Canaries as governor in the hope that he would do less damage there. From the Canaries, Franco took off for North Africa, the launching pad for the insurgent right-wing attack.

Three years later his armies had triumphed in a ruthless struggle that cost around a million Spanish lives. The Canaries were not spared the horrors of the war (mass Republican executions took place in the aptly named Barranco del Infierno, the Gorge of Hell, on Tenerife), but on the whole the islands prospered during Franco's dictatorship (which lasted until his death in 1975) and which provided added protection for their free-port status.

Tourism

The massive growth of tourism in the islands since the 1960s has, in some cases, literally refaced the landscape, with brand-new resorts such as Playa de las Américas on Tenerife and Playa del Inglés on Gran Canaria, springing up like Gold Rush boom towns. However, such developments, although they have given the Canaries their current image, are the exception. Whole swathes of even the more developed islands are virtually untouched, while La Palma, La Gomera and El Hierro have only in recent years started

This view of the Castle at Garachico showcases Tenerife's natural beauty.

to provide even the most basic tourist facilities. The infrastructure and transport systems both within and between the islands have, as a consequence, improved drastically.

In 1972 the passing of the Régimen Económico y Fiscal (Economic and Tax Regime) allowed for different methods of tax collection and economic management from that of the rest of Spain. Three years later, after the death of Franco, a constitutional monarchy was restored under Juan Carlos I. However, the subsequent decolonisation of Spain's Western Saharan possessions resulted in a movement of many thousands of people back to the Canary Islands, creating social and logistical problems. The declaration of a new Spanish

The memorial at Santa Cruz.

Constitution in 1978 further strengthened the new democracy and prepared the way for a Statute of Autonomous Regions. In 1982 the Canary Islands were given autonomous status, with many governmental functions transferred from Madrid to the Cabildo Insular, and the status of capital shared between Santa Cruz de Tenerife and Las Palmas de Gran Canaria. Each island has its own local Cabildo (Council) and officials are elected by free vote every four years. In 1986 Spain became part of the EEC (now European Union); this brought the end of the Canary Islands' duty-free port status, but certain special allowances were negotiated. The islands were fully integrated into the EU in 1995.

Despite the economic benefits that tourism has brought, local authorities became aware of the dangers of unchecked development and a 'lager lout' image. Recently there has been an emphasis on a new image for the tourist industry. Ancient paths *(caminos rurales)* have been opened up in the central peaks of Gran Canaria and the northeast of Tenerife, and EU funds have helped promote *turismo rural*, creating country hotels and helping convert traditional buildings into holiday accommodation. All this is part of a drive to encourage conservation-conscious tourism and attract people with a love of the countryside, as well as those seeking fun, sun and sand.

WHERE TO GO

TENERIFE

Tenerife is the largest of the Canaries, with an area of some 2,045 sq km (790 sq miles) and a population of 700,000. It offers the visitor more sights, more attractions, more towns and cities to explore and more contrasts than any of the other islands, from banana plantations to sandy beaches and snow-capped mountains. Tenerife has been welcoming visitors from cold northern climes since the 19th century. However, the focus has changed from the cloudy, green north coast where Puerto de la Cruz was once the favourite resort (it is still enormously popular), to the hot, arid south.

Santa Cruz de Tenerife

Santa Cruz, the capital of Tenerife, the principal port and the administrative centre for the westerly Canaries, is not a city in which tourists spend a great deal of time. However, there are some pleasant parks and squares, a lively shopping and eating area and a number of interesting museums and churches. The main square is the **Plaza de España,** in the middle of which stands the **Monumento de los Caídos**, a memorial to the dead of the Spanish Civil War. The Art Deco building beside it, with a clock tower, is the **Cabildo Insular** (island government headquarters); it also houses the post office, and the tourist office is next door. The **Calle del Castillo**, the principal shopping street, heads inland from the square. Off to the right is the **Museo Municipal de Bellas Artes** (open Tues–Fri 10am–8pm, Sat–Sun 10am–2pm; free) which has some impressive pictures. Further north, up Calle San Francisco, is the **Museo Militar** (open Tues–Sat 10am–2pm; admission fee) which houses El Tigre, the cannon from which the shot that shattered Admiral Nelson's arm in 1797 was allegedly fired.

Heading south, the **Instituto Óscar Domínguez de Arte y Cultura Contemporanea**, near the **Teatro Guimerá**, designed by Tate Modern architects Herzog & De Meuron, opens in 2005 . Beside the Barranco de Santos, stands the **Iglesia de Nuestra Señora de la Concepción** (Church of the Immaculate Conception). Dating from the early 16th century, this is the town's most important historical building and contains several interesting relics, including Admiral Nelson's faded battle flag. On the other side of the *barranco* (a dry river bed) is the **Museo de la Naturaleza y el Hombre** (open Tues–Sun 9am–7pm; admission fee), with exhibits illustrating the lives and the death rituals of Guanche society; and the **Mercado de Nuestro Señora de Àfrica**, a colourful fruit, flower and vegetable market.

Santa Cruz's sleek new Auditorio.

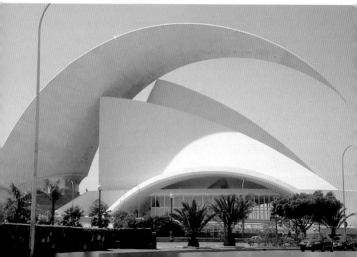

On the main highway near the port stands the elegant new **Auditorio**, a concert hall designed by Basque architect Santiago Calatrava, which is home to the Tenerife Symphony Orchestra. Beside it is a new bus station and behind it, beyond the old **Castillo San Juan**, is the **Parque Marítimo César Manrique** (open daily 9am– 5pm; admission fee), an area of sea-water pools, with trees, flowers and waterfalls.

North of the city lies the **Playa de las Teresitas**, the city beach, a long stretch of golden sand, imported from the Sahara in the 1970s.

Puerto de la Cruz

Puerto de la Cruz has been attracting northern Europeans for over a century and it maintains much of its colonial grandeur. The seafront promenade has been quite heavily commercialised but not spoiled, and the atmosphere is always lively without being boisterous. The main square, the **Plaza del Charco de los Camarones** (Square of the Shrimp Pool), is the hub of both tourist and local life, and the cafés, restaurants and shops are busy at all hours.

Just off the square, the old town around the **Puerto Pesquero** is remarkably oblivious to change. Among the narrow streets, with faded wooden balconies and carved doors, are the 18th-century **Casa de Miranda**, which now houses a craft shop and restaurant (the Bodiquita); and, facing the tiny port the **Casa de la Real Aduana** (Customs House), the oldest building in town, dating from 1620.

Nearby (going west) you will come to the Hotel Monopol one of Puerto's oldest, with beautiful balconies; and, in the Plaza de la Iglesia, the town's principal church, **Iglesia de Nuestra Señora de la Penna de Francia**, built in 1697.

The problem of lack of a decent beach in Puerto was brilliantly addressed by the late César Manrique (the Lanzarote

Frisky dolphins at Loro Parque.

artist who died in 1992). He designed **Lago Martiánez** (open daily 9am–5pm; admission fee), a 3-hectare (8-acre) complex of tropical lagoons, cascading fountains and sunbathing terraces, cleverly landscaped with lush palms and black-and-white volcanic rocks to fit perfectly into the seafront, where the surf crashes spectacularly against the rocks. The Lago is also known as the Lido San Telmo because the gleaming white Iglesia de San Telmo, dedicated to sailors, stands nearby.

Just to the west of Puerto is **Loro Parque** (open daily 9am–6pm; admission fee), with what may be the world's largest collection of parrots – more than 300 species. It is home to an eclectic array of creatures, including chimpanzees, alligators and sea-lions. There is also an aquarium and shark tunnel, a splendid dolphinarium, and Planet Penguin, a natural habitat for the penguins.

Just north of Puerto, on the road to La Orotavo, there are two places that have similar themes, but exhibit them in rather different ways. The oldest of these, and closest to town, is the **Jardín Botánico** (Botanical Garden; open summer: daily 9am–7pm; winter: 9am–6pm; admission fee), founded by royal decree in 1788. Covering some 2.5 hectares (6 acres), it has palms of every variety and the centrepiece is a huge South

American fig tree whose enormous branches and roots have become intertwined into one great tree house.

Further on, the **Bananera El Guanche** (open daily 9am–6pm; admission fee) provides fascinating insight into how a banana plantation operates. There's a multi-lingual introductory video show, an informative and entertaining brochure plus numerous exhibits in its 1.2-hectare (3-acre) park, which has a superb collection of exotic trees, shrubs, flowers and cacti from all over the world, as well as bananas.

La Orotava

La Orotava is a remarkably well-preserved, unspoiled old town set on a steep hill above Puerto de la Cruz. Stately mansions, ancient churches and cobbled streets are its trademarks. The twin towers, baroque façade and Byzantine dome of the **Iglesia de Nuestra Señora de la Concepción** (rebuilt after earthquake damage in 1705) dominate a skyline that has changed little for centuries. Continue up Calle San Francisco to the splendid, 17th-century **Casa de los Balcones**. The balconies are in the courtyard and are some of the finest of their kind. The house has long been associated with lace making, and assistants in traditional costume will show you what's on offer, and hope that you will buy.

Painting with Sand

To celebrate the feast of Corpus Christi in June, detailed and quite extraordinary works of art are made by spreading multi-coloured volcanic rock and sand particles on the ground in the same way that a conventional artist would spread paint onto a canvas. The plaza in front of the Palacio Municipal in La Orotava is the site for the most acclaimed piece of artwork. Similar pictures are created with flowers and leaves in La Laguna and a few other towns.

Garachico's peninsula, formed by a volcanic eruption.

The **Casa del Turista**, opposite, is almost as grand, and is part of the same outlet for island wares and lace. Also worth visiting is the **Museo de Cerámica** (open 10am–6pm, Sun 10am–4pm; admission fee) in Casa Tafuriaste, a studio and showroom with a collection of traditional Spanish ceramics.

Going North

El Sauzal is important for its wines. Signs lead to the **Casa del Vino La Baranda** (open Tues–Sat 11am–8pm, Sun and holidays 11am–6pm; admission fee). You can see how the wine is made, then enjoy tastings and make purchases from the shop. There is a bar and restaurant, with fine views over the coast. **Tacoronte**, nearby, is renowned for a venerated 17th-century figure of Christ, **Cristo de los Dolores** (Christ of Sorrows), in the monastery church in the Plaza del Cristo.

La Laguna

La Laguna, declared a UNESCO World Heritage Site in 1999, is Tenerife's second-largest town, known as the cultural capital of the island; there has been a university here since 1701. Start at the **Plaza del Adelantado**, behind which is the Mercado de San Miguel (especially lively on Saturday and Sunday morning). On the square, the neo-classical **Ayuntamiento** (Town Hall) and the baroque **Palacio de Nava** are two secular highlights. In between is the massive **Iglesia-Convento de Santa Catalina de Siena**, with an ornate Canarian balcony. A short way along Calle Obispo Rey Redondo is the **Cathedral** (Santa Iglesia), with twin bell towers. The original, 16th-century building fell into disrepair, and this one was built between 1904 and 1913. Continue along the street to the town's oldest church, the **Iglesia de Nuestra Señora de la Concepción** built in 1502. Its seven-storey belfry and watchtower were added two centuries later. The interior is outstanding, with exquisite timber carvings on the ceiling, pulpit and choir stalls. The font was used to baptise converted Guanche leaders. You can see the interior of an historic mansion in Calle San Agustin, where Casa Lercaro houses the **Museo de Historia y Archivo Insular** (open Tues–Sun 9am– 7pm; admission fee).

West of Puerto

A day's outing from Puerto de la Cruz along the unspoiled north and west coasts covers some of the island's most spectacular sights and scenery. Sleepy Icod de Los Vinos is the home of the botanical freak that is **Drago Milenario**, a huge dragon tree *(Draecana draco)* reputed to be 1,000 years old.

Continue west on the coast road from Icod to **Garachico** and after 6km (3½ miles) the tortuous descent begins. There are marvellous views down onto this compact little town of

6,000 inhabitants, set on a small peninsula with waves crashing all around. The peninsula was formed from the volcanic debris deposited by an eruption in 1709, when most of the town and its inhabitants were destroyed. The best viewpoints are the **Mirador de Garachico** and the beautifully preserved, 16th-century **Castillo de San Miguel**. A lucky survivor, this fortress, with heraldic arms above the door, now houses a bar and restaurant. There is no beach to speak of, but a cleverly designed set of pools built into the rocks more than compensates. Despite the destruction, Garachico is a little gem. Neat houses with attractive balconies line cobbled streets and old churches adorn pretty squares. Another survivor of the earthquake is the 16th-century convent of Francis of Assisi, which now houses the Casa de la Cultura, while a museum of contemporary art is housed in the 17th-century former convent of Santo Domingo.

Offshore, the oddly shaped, lava stone **Roque de Garachico** has been designated a natural monument, and serves as a refuge for endangered species of seabirds.

About 8 km (5 miles) along the coast road, past Buenavista del Norte, lies the most westerly point on Tenerife, the **Punta de Teno**. From here there are panoramic views across to La Gomera and south to the massive cliffs of Los Gigantes. Turn back to Buenavista and take a marked turn inland to Masca. Be warned, though, that this is not a drive to be undertaken by inexperienced or nervous drivers.

Initially the road, climbing up the arable hillsides, is no problem, but this soon changes once the entrance to the vertiginous valley is reached. Until this road was built in 1991 the picturesque village of **Masca** could only be reached on the back of a donkey. All around is some of the most dramatic scenery on the island, but if you are driving, you won't have any time to savour it. The road clings precariously to the side of lush, green mountains cleft by deep, dark ravines and often zig-zags on itself in the tightest of hairpin bends. And it is not unknown to have to reverse back down and around these bends, allowing other vehicles to pass. A stop at Masca is not just a pleasure, but also a relief. Relax at one of the restaurants en route and enjoy the stupendous scenery before continuing south on an equally difficult drive, to re-join the main road at Santiago del Teide.

A little further south, turn off towards the resort of **Puerto de Santiago** (which has a good beach) then walk out to the edge of the marina jetty to get the best view of the enormous sheer cliffs, up to 800m (2,625ft) high, which are appropriately known as **Los Gigantes** (The Giants). A small port of the same name has developed into a busy resort. It is a popular diving centre *(see What to Do, page 81)* and, although there is only a small, black sand beach, you can swim in an artificial sea water lido.

The Central Area

There are four main roads up to the **Parque Nacional de las Cañadas del Teide**, so it is always accessible, wherever you are on the island. The park is well sign-posted from the road via La

Spectacular rock formations in the National Park.

Orotava, but if you are coming from the north the most picturesque route is via **La Esperanza**. The small town soon gives way to a lush forest of giant pines and eucalyptus trees, the Bosque de La Esperanza. Four km (2½ miles) south at **Las Raíces** is where Franco met with his co-conspirators in 1936 *(see page 20)*. An obelisk commemorates the event. As the road gains altitude and temperatures fall, the views become ever more spectacular. The gleaming white towers you see off to the east belong to the **Observatorio Astronómico del Teide** (open Wed and Fri 10am–2pm by appointment only; tel: 922 605 200). It was begun in 1965, but increasing light pollution on the island has since affected its usefulness.

> The bleak landscape here is often described as lunar and it was the site for some of the filming for *Planet of the Apes* in 1966.

The entrance to the National Park is **El Portillo**, where there is a Visitor Centre (open daily 9am–4pm), well stocked with videos and information about daily signposted and guided walks. A road running through the park is dotted with *miradors* (viewing points) offering spectacular views. Unless you are up for a five-hour climb, the last part of the journey to the summit (**Pico del Teide**) has to be made by **Teleférico** (cable car), 8km (5miles) south of the visitor centre, and close to the **Parador Nacional del Teide**, the only accommodation in the park. Arrive early in the morning at the Teleférico to avoid queues and be aware that it does not operate in windy weather. El Teide, the highest mountain in Spain, is 3,718m (12,198ft) above sea level and it is extremely cold. Snow caps it for most of the year and temperatures can be well below freezing.

Most people who alight from the cable car do not want to walk far, and anyone who suffers from coronorary or respiratory problems should not attempt to do so, as there is 50 percent less oxygen in the air than at sea level. You can walk to the rim of the crater, but to prevent erosion, the authorities have introduced a system whereby you need a permit to do so. They are available free from the Parque Nacional office, Calle Emilio Calzadillo 5, Santa Cruz (tel: 922 290 129; Mon–Fri 9am–2pm). You will need your passport and you will also need to show it when you are at the summit.

El Teide rises from a great hollow, a *caldera*, that is the remnant of an earlier, much larger volcano. In fact there were two earlier volcanoes, creating two *calderas*, separated by the extraordinary

Date palms are commonly seen on the island.

gnarled formations of **Los Roques de García**, close to the Parador. Lava and ashes have spilled from the volcanoes in a series of eruptions at different times, which explains why the rocks are so varied in texture and colour. Some of those in an area near Los Roques are deep green from copper oxide, and are known as **Los Azulejos** (The Tiles). A left turn at the **Mirador Boca de Tauce** a little further on will take you out of the park, down to the village of Vilaflor. Or you could continue to the Mirador de Chío for a stark, cindery view of **Las Narices del Teide** (El Teide's Nostrils) created by an eruption in 1798.

The East

Candelaria, about 17km (11 miles) south of Santa Cruz, is a town with deep religious roots. It is dominated by the over-sized 1950s **basilica** (open daily 7.30am–1pm, 3–7.30pm; free), containing an image of the Virgin, who, according to legend, was washed ashore here and worshipped by the Guanches, well before Christianity came to the Canaries. The statue and an earlier church were destroyed in 1826 when a tidal wave reclaimed the Virgin, the patron saint of the Canary Islands. The splendid new statue is the object of a major two-day pilgrimage in mid-August, the **Romería de Nuestra Señora de la Candelaria**, when the conversion of the Guanches to Christianity is re-enacted. Lining the sea side of the basilica's square are statues of the seven Guanche *menceys*, or chiefs, who were in power at the time of the Spanish conquest.

Just south and inland from Candelaria is the little working town of **Güímar**. Some of the dry stone terraces around the town, known as *molleros* or *majones*, look like the bases of pyramids and it is no surprise to find the **Parque Etno-gráfico Pirámides de Güímar** (open daily 9.30m–6pm; admission fee) above the town. This park is the work of Thor Heyerdahl, who lived in Tenerife from 1994 until his death in 2002. During that time Heyerdahl, who had done exten-sive research on the pyramids of Tucume in Peru, discovered what he believed to be the Guanches' cult of building flat-topped, step-sided pyramids for sun worship, similar to those found on both sides of the Atlantic. Shipowner and fellow Norwegian, Fred Olsen, bought the land for the park and helped to develop it into a centre of research (check <www.fredolsen.es/piramides> for more details).On view are models of Heyerdahl's vessels, a video detailing his sum-maries and trans-oceanic crossings and various other audiovisual displays, as well as the pyramids themselves. There is still controversy about the authenticity of the pyramids, but it is well worth visiting the site and deciding for yourself.

The South Coast

The most popular tourist destinations in Tenerife are the adjacent resorts of **Los Cristianos** and **Playa de las Américas**. The former used to be a small fishing port with a quiet little beach. It now plays host to hundreds of thousands of visitors each year. Traces of the old town can still be found around the

Plenty of diversions in Playa de las Américas.

port, though it is difficult to locate anything but British or German bars and restaurants along the crowded beachfront. The port is still active, its ferries serving the neighbouring islands of El Hierro and La Gomera. The south-facing **Playa los Cristianos** and **Playa de las Vistas** are sheltered, and the sea shallow and safe.

Los Cristianos is separated from its neighbour by the volcanic cone of Montaña Chayofila, but it is otherwise hard to see the join. Playa de las Américas was born in the 1970s and has quickly developed from a bare shoreline to the high-rise, high-energy, highly packaged resort it is today. It has no natural centre or heart, the roads are often not signposted and directions are generally given by the names of

Take a trip on a yellow submarine.

hotels. A large beach, the Playa de Las Vistas, lies between the ambitious **Mare Nostrum** hotel resort and Los Cristianos, but the main beaches of **Playas de Troya** and **Playa del Bobo** are on the north side of the **Barranco del Rey**. There is a tourist information point beside this *barranco* (ravine), which is near the rowdy strip called **Veronicas**, hub of more than 100 discos and nightclubs.

On the other side of Playa de las Américas, but with a border as indistinguishable as that with Los Cristianos, is the newly popular area of **Costa Adeje**. Here, the wall-to-wall hotels, fast food joints and amusement arcades give way to spacious, cleverly designed resort hotels offering extensive facilities and creating a more agreeable ambience than that of its two near neighbours.

The small harbour of **Puerto Colón** in San Eugenio is the centre for water-based activities – glass-bottomed boat trips, and dolphin- and whale-watching boats *(see What To Do, page 87)*. The **Yellow Submarine** will take you under the ocean on a 45-minute trip that is especially interesting when it passes wrecks on the sea bed which have become a haven for fish, notably an array of huge stingrays. Inland from the port is a large **Aquapark**.

EL HIERRO

El Hierro, the smallest and most southwesterly of the Canary Islands, with an area of 280 sq km (110 sq miles), is in the administrative province of Santa Cruz de Tenerife. It has the highest density of volcanoes in the archipelago, although the last eruption was over 200 years ago. There are more than 500 cones on the surface, with an additional 300 covered by lava flows. It has few tourist facilities and no good beaches, but it is quiet, pretty and totally unspoiled – and some of the scenery is extraordinarily dramatic. A good road links the airport, the port and the capital, Valverde, then switchbacks across the island to El Golfo, but this journey has been made much faster and easier (if less scenic) by the construction of the Moncanal tunnel that now links the capital with Frontera. Minor roads lead to most points of interest, but none go all the way round the coast. Visitors arrive at the airport on domestic flights from Tenerife or Gran Canaria, or by boat at Puerto de la Estaca.

Exploring the Island

Both entry points are close to **Valverde**, the only Canarian capital located inland, which was built 700m (2,300ft) above sea level to protect it from pirate raids. It is a small town, centred on the church of Nuestra Señora de la Concepción. There's not a lot to see – although you could visit the Casa de las Quinteras (open Mon–Fri 9am–2pm) to see local crafts and industry – but there's a cheerful atmosphere, lots of bars and a few good restaurants. You can get a bus from the bus station to other parts of the island. If you are driving, you could take the scenic route over the high spine of the island, across the *meseta*, to the farming town of San Andrés, then on to the cliff-top **Mirador de la Peña** at the northern end of **El Golfo**. The cliffs were once part of an immense volcanic crater, but some 50,000 years ago one side of it slid into the sea, leaving behind a fertile valley and a gigantic bay. From the *mirador* restaurant, designed by César Manrique, there are dramatic views.

The chapel of Nuestra Señora de los Reyes.

Alternatively, drive through the new Moncanal tunnel from Valverde to **Frontera**, a village that is known mainly for its church of Nuestra Señora de la Candelaria, with a free-standing bell-tower set on a volcanic cone, and the adjacent *lucha canaria* stadium *(see page 84)*. On the coast close by is the **Lagartario** (open Jul–Sept: Tues–Sun 10.30am–2.30pm, 5–7pm; Oct–May: Tues–Sat; admission fee), where specimens of El Hierro's giant lizards are cared for, and the **Ecomuseo de Guinea** (open Tues–Sat 10.30am–2.30pm, 5–7pm, Sun 11am–2pm; admission fee), a restored village that shows developments in rural dwellings from the time of the Spanish conquest to the 20th century.

West of here lie the pretty village of **Sabinosa**, the remote Santuario de Nuestra Señora de los Reyes, and **El Sabinal**, a forest of juniper trees *(sabinosas)*, twisted, gnarled and, in some cases, almost bent double by the wind. Close by, but difficult to reach, is **Punta Orchilla**, the site of the zero meridian before it was transferred to Greenwich in the 19th century. This used to be considered the edge of the known world, and it certainly seems like it. From here there's a poor road to the best beach, **Playa del Verodal**.

To reach the southeastern point of the island, return to the central axis then drop down through gentle pastures and pine woods to the village of **El Pinar**, known for ceramics and jewellery. The route then runs through inhospitable volcanic clinker to **La Restinga**, a fishing village with a black sand beach, a diving centre and some good fish restaurants. The neighbouring **Bahía de Naos** is a marine nature reserve.

LA GOMERA

The circular island of **La Gomera**, also part of the province of Santa Cruz de Tenerife, is 378 sq km (147 sq miles) in area with a population of 16,000, twice that of El Hierro. It is a rugged, mountainous island, its coastline dominated by dramatic cliffs. There are few beaches and the interior is full of vertiginous, mostly verdant, valleys, lined with narrow fields stepped into the mountainsides. These valleys are often covered by a ceiling of cloud, whisked in by the trade winds, which seem to hang perpetually over the island.

In the centre, the Parque Nacional de Garajonay *(see page 42)*, is a dense area of forest and fauna. In fact, a third of this little island has been divided into 17 UNESCO-designated protected areas. Such terrain makes it difficult to get around. Roads twist and turn, often looping back on themselves in hairpin bends. Road surfaces are improving, but many are still of poor quality and road signs leave much to be desired.

La Gomera is reached by ferry or domestic flights from neighbouring islands. The airport is in the south, near Playa de Santiago, the port is San Sebastián, the island capital.

San Sebastián

San Sebastián (pop. 6.200) is a small town, known as the place where Columbus stopped to stock up with fresh food and water before leaving the known world in September

The Lady in the Tower

The Torre del Conde (Tower of the Count) lies to the west of the main square. It is named after Count Hernán Peraza, who was ambushed and murdered one night at a mountain pass by two Guanche chiefs as he returned from an assignation with a Guanche princess. His wife, Beatriz, took refuge in the tower and legend has it that she entertained Columbus here before he set off on his voyage of discovery. The building does not seem to have changed much in the subsequent centuries.

The harbour in San Sebastián.

1492. The Columbiana starts in the main square, the **Plaza de las Américas**. A pavement mosaic shows the route of Columbus's voyage and next to the large tree is the Casa de Aduana (Customs House). It is said that Columbus drew water from the well here and took it to the New World. Leading off the square, the **Calle del Medio**, the only street of any consequence, features more connections with the great navigator. The **Iglesia de la Virgen de la Asunción**, built between 1490 and 1510, looks and feels so old that you can easily imagine Columbus praying in a dark recess, as a plaque here tells us he did, in 1492. A little way up the street is the modest **Casa de Colón** (open Mon–Fri 10am–1pm, 4–6pm; free), which is supposedly where the navigator stayed while in La Gomera. Restored by the local authorities, it displays some pre-Columbian pottery from Latin America and items relating to Columbus's voyage.

The North

The road from San Sebastián climbs steeply and the views soon become quite dizzying. The highest peak on La Gomera, **Alto de Garajonay** is 1,487m (4,878ft) – this is no great height by Canaries standards, yet the island often gives the impression of being a fearsome maze of eerie crags. The small town of **Hermigua** is the largest on the island after San Sebastián. Stop at the crafts centre of **Los Telares** to look down into its green and fertile valley and ask if you can try the local liqueur, *mistela*, while watching women making blankets and rugs on their antique looms. Next comes **Agulo**, a pleasant little town perched precipitously on a headland. Its main feature (part from the location) is the domed Iglesia San Marco, originally a mosque, which stands beside a monumental laurel tree in the plaza.

A turn inland just before the village of Las Rosas takes you into the **Parque Nacional de Garajonay**, which was declared a UNESCO World Heritage Site in 1986. The **Juego de Bolas Visitors Centre** (open Tues–Sun 9.30am–4.30pm) incorporates a small Ethnographic Museum and a herbal garden and has lots of information on the park.

The road then continues through the 3,984-hectare (9,884-acre) park to **La Laguna Grande** restaurant, a hospitable, rough-and-ready sort of place, which is very popular with walkers.

There are no views from here, except at Garajonay itself, and an almost perpetual mist clings to the ancient, moss-covered trees. As there is little rainfall on La Gomera this mist, spawned by the trade winds, assumes great ecological importance, having given life to this sub-tropical forest, which includes laurel, cedar, juniper and olive trees, swathed in ferns and ephiphytes (plants that derive their nutrients from the air).

*The road into Valle Gran Rey twists back and forth
through the lush countryside.*

The South

Starting the trip south from San Sebastián, the road leads
past three mighty volcanic plugs to the windy pass of
Degollada de Peraza, which offers spectacular views to
both north and south; this is where the road divides. Instead
of going in the direction of Garajonay, turn left on an
extremely winding road that leads to **Playa de Santiago**
(and the airport).

Apart from San Sebastián this is one of the few waterside
communities on the island. There is a small port and a peb-
bly little beach but the main event is to be found on the cliffs
immediately to the east. Here, the Norwegian shipping mag-
nate Fred Olsen has created the **Jardín Tecina**, an upmar-
ket resort with accommodation in a series of white,
Canarian-style villas.

*Serious sunbathers at
Playa Gran Rey.*

Retrace your route, passing the airport, and at Igualero turn left (west) on to a minor road to Las Hayas. Stop in the village of **El Cercado** where ceramic items are still made in the traditional manner by hand, without a potter's wheel. You can watch the potters at work then be tempted to purchase the results. You may be surprised by the prices, which are nearly as steep as the island's cliffs and valley.

From Las Hayas continue along to the main road at Arure where, immediately after turning left, there is a small bodega selling wines from La Gomera and the rest of the Canary Islands. La Gomera has about 300 hectares (742 acres) of vineyards, mostly cultivated on uneven land with steep slopes and small terraces. A stop at the highest point, at the combined mirador/restaurant Escuela César Manrique, will give you stupendous views of the verdant **Valle Gran Rey**, a deep and fertile gorge that has been terraced and planted with a wide variety of fruit and vegetables, and has been colonised by laid-back northern Europeans seeking peace and tranquillity.

Where the valley reaches the sea, the pretty village of **La Calera**, set on a hill, has a number of boutiques and restaurants; and the little town of **Valle Gran Rey** has a black-sand beach, a few bars and restaurants and a dive centre. Return through the valley, continue past Arure and then take a right turn at the T-junction which will lead you along the southern edge of the national park and back to San Sebastián.

LA PALMA

La Palma, the most northwesterly of the Canaries, has an area of 725 sq km (280 sq miles) and a population of 81,500. It has two nicknames – La Isla Bonita (The Beautiful Island) and La Isla Verde (The Green Island) and both are appropriate. Its statistics are impressive, too. The highest peak, Roque de los Muchachos, rises 2,423m (7,950ft) above sea level, making it the steepest island in the world in relation to its total area. It is also the only one of the Canary Islands to have any streams – even very small ones.

Santa Cruz de la Palma

Santa Cruz de la Palma, the island capital, is an appealing town – clean and bright with traditional and modern architecture side-by-side creating a pleasing atmosphere. Most people agree that it is the most attractive of the Canary Islands' capitals. The prestige of the town was such that, during the Renaissance era, it was the third most important port of the Spanish Empire, after Sevilla and Antwerp.

The heart of the town is the triangular **Plaza de España**, set a couple of streets in from the seafront on the Calle Real. On one side of the triangle is the **Iglesia Matriz del Salvador** (Church of the Saviour), built in 1503. The intricate wooden panelled ceiling of this big stone church is a fine example of the *mudéjar* style, a mixture of Muslim and Christian-Gothic elements perfected by the Muslim craftsmen who chose to remain in Spain after the 15th-century reconquest. Beside the church, the **Casa Monte Verde**, dating from 1618 but rebuilt in the 1920s, is the most notable of the splendid 18th-century colonial-style mansions.

The longest side of the triangle is taken up by the colonnaded **Ayuntamiento** (Town Hall), built between 1559 and 1567 with stone brought from La Gomera; this is considered the most important Renaissance building in the Canary Islands. While the arches are Italian Renaissance, the interior (which you are free to inspect) is Spanish colonial, with formidable carved wooden ceilings and doors and a ceremonial staircase with frescoes painted in the mid-20th century.

The **Calle Real** is a delightful street in which to stroll and enjoy the atmosphere. At its southern end it takes on the improbable name of Calle O'Daly, after an Irish banana merchant who settled on the island. On the parallel Avenida Marítimo, you will find the wonderful row of old houses known as the **Casas de los Balcones**. Built in the 19th century, they have become symbolic of Santa Cruz. Colourful and characteristic, with a Portuguese influence, they take their name from their overhanging balconies; the houses facing the sea were once used as lookout posts.

Among other points of interest is the **Iglesia de San Francisco**, in the square of the same name, with a *mudéjar* ceiling to equal that in the church of El Salvador. The cloister now houses the **Museo Insular** (open Mon–Fri 9am–2pm, 4–6.30pm; admission fee), with an eclectic mixture of exhibits. At the end of Calle Pérez Brito is **El Barco de la Virgen**, a life-size replica of Columbus's ship, *Santa María*, which houses the **Museo Naval** (open Mon–Fri 9.30am–2pm, 4–6.30pm; admission fee).

Santa Cruz also has a lively market, the **Mercado Municipal**, selling local produce; and two castles, the Castillo Real, in the town itself and the Castillo de la Virgen, on a promontory above.

*The colourful Casas de los Balcones have become
a symbol of Santa Cruz.*

Due to the steep, dorsal shape of the island there are only two main island routes to follow: the loop south of the Caldera de Taburiente and the loop north of it. The southern route is the more interesting of the two.

The Southern Loop

Heading west from Santa Cruz the first stop of interest is **Las Nieves**, a village built on the mountainside. You will first come to a roadside bar, then the 17th-century **Real Santuario de Nuestra Señora de las Nieves** (Sanctuary of Our Lady of the Snows), repository of the venerated 14th-century terracotta image of the Virgen de las Nieves, who is said to have appeared in Rome during an August snowstorm.

The Virgin is celebrated every year on 5 August, but every five years (2005, 2010, etc.) there is a special event, when the image is carried to Santa Cruz in a procession known as *La Bajada de la Virgen* (The Descent of the Virgin).

Heading west, the road dives into a tunnel cut through La Cumbre Nueva, the mountainous ridge that runs though the centre of the island. At the other side, you pass the the Centro de Visitantes of the Parque Nacional de la Caldera de Taburiente *(see page 51)*. The main road then continues west to El Paso, a sweet village with traditional houses surrounded by a riot of prickly pear cacti. The **Parque Paraíso de las Aves** (open daily 10am–6pm; admission fee) lies just beyond. The park shelters endangered species of exotic birds in lush sur-

Hikers in a La Palma forest take full advantage of the natural beauty of 'the green island'.

roundings, and runs guided tours and educational pro-grammes. The next place of interest, Los Llanos de Aridane, in the heart of a fertile valley, has some good Canarian architecture and a lush, colourful gardens. Just before you reach it, stop at a public garden, the **Pueblo Parque** (open Mon–Sat 10.30am–5pm; admission fee), full of sub-tropical plants.

Before taking the road to the southern tip, make a short detour to the **Mirador El Time**, a lookout point and restaurant perched above a rift valley, where the views are stupendous; then drop down to **Tazacorte**, a pretty village and harbour with some good fish restaurants. This was the port where Alonso Fernández de Lugo, the Spanish conqueror, landed in 1492.

Take the main road south now, following the mountain side, to **Fuencaliente**, famous for its wines. There is a winding road, through hills, covered with flowers in spring, to the lighthouse, El Faro de Fuencaliente, at the most southerly tip of La Palma. The first stop is at the **Bodegas Carballo** (open daily 8am–8pm; free; tel: 922 444 140), where you can sample and purchase some surprisingly strong local wines. In 1677 the nearby volcano, San Antonio, erupted, covering once-fertile land with ash, leaving a layer of lapilli approximately 2m (6½ft) deep. By the end of that century farmers had developed a technique of digging trenches that enabled them to reach the fertile layer of earth found under the cinders, where they planted the vines that were then covered with the extracted ashes. This somehow allowed the plants to resist adverse weather conditions and even *phylloxera*, the plant louse that destroyed vines all over Europe in the late 19th century.

Just across the road you can stop at the edge of the crater of **Volcán de San Antonio** (open daily 8am–6pm) and visit the mirador beyond it. In an exposed, windy location this looks quite benign, considering the damage it did. Just south of here are even more recent signs of volcanic activity; the volcano of **Teneguía** that erupted in 1971, fortunately without human casualties. These eruptions sent an ever-widening stream of molten lava rushing down the hillside here and you can see it now, petrified and black, as the road runs right through it. Surprisingly, *plátanos* (bananas) seem to like this environment and can be seen thriving all around you. Once down to sea level you will come across the **Playa de Zamora** a small beach of jet-black sand squeezed in between the surrealistic lava fields. A short distance away, next to the twin lighthouses, is a little fishermen's cove with a stony beach where there is a tiny restaurant – a shack that survived the destruction – that serves delicious fresh fried fish *(see page 138)*.

Heading back towards Santa Cruz, stop at the **Cueva de Belmaco** and the **Parque Arqueológico de Belmaco** (open Mon–Sat 10am–6pm, Sun 10am–2pm; admission fee). The first stone engravings found in the Canary Islands were discovered here in the 18th century, and the 10 natural cave dwellings, with their magnificent rock engravings, were the home to the Benahoritas – the ancient settlers of Benahoare, the aboriginal name for La Palma.

A little further on is **Mazo**, the place to buy authentic-looking replicas of the aboriginal pots, as well as locally-made cigars – *puros*. At Corpus Christi (mid-June) the streets of Mazo are covered in patterned carpets of flowers, leaves and sand.

The Northern Loop

The serpentine road up the east coast runs through some pretty scenery, and you can stop at the **Mirador de San Bartolomé** for beautiful vistas along the coast in both directions. Head next for the seaside village of **San Andrés** with natural swimming pools nearby at **El Charco Azul**

*Santa Cruz de la Palma has attractive architecture,
a beach and a mountain backdrop.*

(The Blue Pool). A little way inland from San Andrés is
the **Bosque de Los Tilos**, a large wooded area that pre-
serves some of the Canary Islands' original, and much de-
pleted, laurel forest. It is a designated Biosphere Reserve
under the protection of UNESCO. There's a **Centro de Visitantes** (open Mon–Fri 9am–5pm) that can provide maps
and information on walking trails.

The main reason to visit the northern part of the island,
however, is the **Parque Nacional de la Caldera de Taburiente**. The Centro de Visitantes (open daily 9am–2pm,
4–6.30pm) is outside the park itself, on the road to El Paso
(see page 48). They have information on the geology and
geomorphology, flora and fauna, and helpful hints on camp-
ing as well as a useful coloured diagram of the hiking trails.

The Caldera de Taburiente is a giant crater, measuring 1,500m (1,640yds) deep, with a diameter of 10km (6 miles). It was created some 400,000 years ago and has since been colonised by nature into a green, fertile valley. From the Visitors' Centre you can drive 7km (4 miles) to the **Mirador La Cumbrecita**, on a road that climbs into a craggy forest surrounded by mist-shrouded peaks with tall pines clinging to the most precarious ledges. There are wonderful views from here (weather permitting – which it doesn't most of the time), including the Roque de los Muchachos and the monolithic Roque Idafe, said to have been the sacred altar of the first Guanche natives on the island. You can enjoy the Caldera by car, but to get the most from the area you have to walk.

Approaching from the north, by road, you must take the turning just outside Santa Cruz that snakes past the Pico de las Nieves to the **Roque de los Muchachos**, the highest point in the island at 2,426m (7,960ft) above sea level. There are several ways up to it, but always be aware of the weather; what looks fine from sea level takes on a different perspective at this height. And, of course, it can change dramatically and quickly, so go prepared with wet-weather gear, warm layers and strong shoes, and be aware that you might not see much but clouds. Besides the views, the other attraction up here is the futuristic **Observatorio Astrofísico** (closed to visitors), regarded as the most important observatory in the Northern Hemisphere and home to some of the world's most important telescopes, including the 400-cm (157-in) William Herschel telescope.

From the observatory, the road continues northwest to the isolated community of **Santo Domingo de Garafía**, where fierce waves lash the rocky coast and you become aware of human frailty when faced with the powers of nature.

GRAN CANARIA

Gran Canaria, the third-largest island in the archipelago, has a great combination of perfect beaches and cultural sites, historic cities and lively nightlife, dramatic scenery and seriously good restaurants. It is almost circular in shape, with an area of 1,530 sq km (590 sq miles) and a coastline of 235km (145 miles), of which more than a fifth consists of beaches, Gran Canaria is the classic volcanic cone in profile and its mountainous character causes the climate to change radically with latitude and altitude. You can leave a damp and cloudy Las Palmas in the early morning and an hour later be enjoying blazing hot sun in Maspalomas.

Gran Canaria is known, with good reason, as a continent in miniature. The coastline ranges from awe-inspiring cliffs to golden dunes. Inland, it varies between stark mountains and tranquil valleys. To preserve this diversity, 32 protected areas cover nearly 43 percent of the island's surface.

Las Palmas

► Bustling **Las Palmas** (population 364,000 – the largest city in the Canaries), is a major commercial and historical centre, a cosmopolitan resort and a vital seaport all rolled into one. It is still one of the busiest ports in the world.

La Playa de las Canteras is Las Palmas' city beach.

The hub of Las Palmas is the **Parque Santa Catalina**, palm-dotted and full of outdoor cafés, buzzing by day and night. On the port side of the park is the striking **Museo Elder** (open Tues–Sun 10am–8pm; admission fee), a wonderful and well-organised science and technology museum. A landscaped pedestrian area leads from the museum to the **Muelle Santa Catalina** where a shiny new commercial centre in brilliant shades of blue and yellow, **El Muelle**, houses stores, cinemas, discos and open-air restaurants and cafés. It is a short walk from the other side of the square to **Playa de las Canteras**, a 3-km (2-mile) stretch of white sand that made the city Gran Canaria's first tourist resort, although it has seen better days and is losing younger tourist trade to the resorts in the south. It is lined with hotels and restaurants, some of which have been here since the 1960s heyday. A wide promenade runs the length of the beach, and a natural reef, **La Barra**, a few hundred metres out, turns this stretch into a natural lagoon, safe for children and non-swimmers.

Take a bus back from Santa Catalina to **Parque Doramas**, a pleasantly landscaped park named after a Guanche chieftain, surrounding the Hotel Catalina. Adjacent to it is the **Pueblo Canario** (Canary Village), a romanticised version of a Canarian village where you can shop for handicrafts and watch displays of folk dancing and singing (Sun 11.30am; free). It was designed by the local Modernist artist, Néstor Fernández de la Torre (1887–1938), and and his architect brother, Miguel. The **Museo Néstor** (open Tues–Sat 10am–8pm, Sun 10.30am–2.30pm; admission fee) displays many of his paintings and stage designs.

Further south is **Parque San Telmo**, where the city's main (underground) bus terminal, a pretty little chapel, the Ermita de San Telmo, and an art nouveau refreshment kiosk,

Apartment blocks on the outskirts of Las Palmas have been brightened up with colourful paintwork.

decorated with gleaming tiles, marks the start of **Triana**, one of the older *barrios* (districts). The long, pedestrianised shopping street of Calle Mayor de Triana, has attractive art nouveau façades and a wide variety of shops. The **Casa-Museo Pérez Galdós** (open Mon–Fri 9am–8pm, sometimes Sat–Sun 10am–1pm; guided tours; free) pays homage to the writer born here in 1843 and known as the Spanish Balzac. The house is a delightful example of Canarian architecture. Close by are two pretty squares, the **Plazoleta de Cairasco**, with the splendid **Gabinete Literario**, an art nouveau treasure designated a 'Monumento Histórico Artistico'; and Hurtado de Mendoza, usually known as **Las Ranas** (The Frogs) because the long pool that runs down the centre is fed by two spouting frogs.

Cross the major highway, Calle Juan de Quesada, and you reach **Vegueta**, the oldest part of the city, where Spanish forces first set up camp in 1478. It is claimed that Christopher Columbus prayed at the **Ermita de San Antonio Abad** before setting off to the New World.

Close by on Calle Colón is the beautiful, 15th-century **Casa de Colón** (open Mon–Fri 9am–7pm, Sat–Sun 9am–3pm; admission fee). This was the residence of the island's first governor and Columbus is said to have stayed here, although there is no evidence to support this. Now an atmospheric museum, with a pretty courtyard, it recreates the Age of Discovery with exhibits of navigational instruments, charts and weapons, a replica of the cabin of *La Niña*, one of Columbus's ships and pre-Columbian artefacts from Mexico and the Ecuadorian island of La Tolita.

Around the corner stands the vast bulk of the **Catedral de Santa Ana** (open Mon–Fri 10am–4.30pm, Sat 10am–1.30pm; access only through Diocesan Museum; admission fee), a mixture of Gothic, Renaissance and neoclassical styles. The adjoining **Museo Diocesano de Arte Sacro** (open as above; entrance in Calle Espíritu Santo) has a lovely cloister, the Patio de los Naranjos (Patio of the Orange Trees), its tranquillity disturbed only by birdsong. A modern lift will whisk you up to the top of one of the cathedral's two towers for a great view over the city.

Facing the cathedral across the **Plaza de Sant Ana** are the splendid Casas Consistoriales (Island Government Offices), which have recently undergone substantial renovation work.

Not far away, the **Centro Atlántico de Arte Moderno (CAAM)** (open Tues–Sat 10am–9pm, Sun 10am–2pm; free) focuses on the work of young Canarian artists. The nearby **Museo Canario** (open Mon–Fri 10am–8pm, Sat–Sun 10am–2pm; admission fee) holds the Canary Islands' most important collection of pre-Hispanic objects, including a room full of Cro-Magnon skulls and mummies.

The East Coast

Heading down the *autopista* (motorway) past the airport to the southern beaches, it is well worth stopping off at the **Barranco de Guayadeque**. Now under a protection order, the *barranco* is one of the most beautiful valleys on the island, its steep slopes are honeycombed with cave dwellings, and lush flora still thrives here. The **Centro de Interpretación** (open Tues–Sat 9am–5pm, Sun 10am–6pm; admission fee) has lots of displays on its history and will give information on hiking trails. The *barranco*

The road through the Barranco de Guayadeque.

is for serious walkers, but the less energetic can drive for some 9km (5 miles) beyond the Interpretation Centre, passing glorious scenery, to reach two cave villages, both still viable communities. The road ends at the best-known cave restaurant, the **Tagoror**.

Nearby, **Agüimes** is one of the most appealing towns on the island. Among the ochre- and terracotta-coloured houses in the spotless, narrow streets, a number of bronze statues have been erected, portraying rural life and local characters. Several houses have been converted into *casa rural* accommodation *(see page 103)*. The neoclassical **Iglesia de San Sebastián** (open daylight hours) at one end of the square, is a designated Monumento Histórico Artístico.

A short way from Agüimes is **Playa de Vargas**, venue for the annual PWA Windsurf Championships; and a marine reserve and diving centre, at **Playa del Cabrón** *(see page 81),*

Southern Exposure

The southern resorts of San Agustín, Playa del Inglés and Maspalomas, the biggest holiday complex in Spain, are synonymous with package holidays. Built in the 1960s to provide instant gratification, they offer year-round good weather, miles of rolling sands, water sports facilities, hotels and apartments with lush gardens and landscaped swimming pools; and restaurants, clubs, bars and shops by the score.

San Agustín , the first resort you reach on the GC-1 motorway, is a relatively restrained area of apartment complexes, catering mainly for retired couples and families with young children, although it is also extremely popular with windsurfers. You can walk along the promenade to **Playa del**

Inglés, a far louder and more robust resort. The name means English Beach, but it attracts numerous German visitors as well. This is a sprawling sun, sea and sand resort of high-rise hotels, shopping malls, amusement arcades and fast-food restaurants. The nightlife at the numerous discos, bars and clubs can be hectic and lasts till the early hours.

Trekking across the dunes at Maspalomas.

➤ **Maspalomas** is separated from Playa del Inglés by a spectacular stretch of **dunes** that cover an area of 4 sq km (1½ sq miles) and were designated a nature reserve in 1994 in order to preserve the ecosystem. You can walk over the dunes if you protect your feet from the hot sand. Adjoining the dunes, a golf course forms another barrier, but inland the two resorts almost merge into each other, although their style is distinctive. Maspalomas is a more up-market resort and accommodation is in smart hotels, bungalows or low-rise apartment complexes set in large, lush gardens. Playa de Maspalomas is the stretch of dunes close to **El Faro**, the lighthouse. From here a palm-lined *paseo* leads to the area known as **El Oasis**, a place of ultra-smart hotels beside **La Charca**, a small lagoon.

There is a plethora of family attractions nearby, all reached by regular bus services from the resorts *(see What to Do, pages 86–87)*. West of Maspalomas the coastline becomes dominated by towering, barren looking cliffs that form natural bays and coves. A new stretch of motorway continues to Puerto Rico, but the coast road passes **Pasito Blanco**, a little port and resort mainly of interest to sailing enthusiasts; and **Arguiniguín**, a working fishing port that has seen quite a bit of tourist development recently.

Puerto Rico is the next major resort on this coast. Conceived in the 1970s it has been somewhat overdeveloped, with a wall of apartment blocks rising to the top of the hills, like tiers of seats in a giant amphitheatre. Its pretty, sheltered beach is clean and family-oriented but can become unbearably crowded. The **Puerto Deportivo** caters for fishing and water sports enthusiasts and for those who just like being on the water. There are diving schools and sailing schools, deep-sea fishing trips, 'dolphin search' trips in glass-bottomed catamarans, or simple pleasure trips that run up and down the coast.

The beach and crowded hillside of Puerto Rico.

Puerto de Mogán is a lesson in how to provide accommodation that is functional, attractive and totally in sympathy with its surroundings. Built round a complex of sea-water canals with delicately arched bridges, the modern versions of traditional local townhouses are ablaze with bougainvillaea and trailing geraniums. There are two ports, the working one, from which a fishing fleet still operates; and the **Puerto Deportivo**, where luxurious yachts bob in the water. The latter is lined with cafés and restaurants, all offering wonderful views and fish and seafood menus, all fairly similar. There is a small, south-facing beach to the east of the port, that has recently been 'sandscaped' and extended. **Submarine Adventure** offers trips in a yellow submarine *(see page 87)* and pleasure boats ply back and forth between here, Puerto Rico and Arguiniguín.

Northern Coast and Hinterland

Going west from Las Palmas on the new stretch of motorway, take the exit for **Arucas**, a workaday town overshadowed by the huge lava-stone church of **San Juan Bautista**; begun in 1909, said to owe its inspiration to Antoni Gaudí's Sagrada Família in Barcelona. The road west from Arucas follows a dizzying route through the mountains, but you can return to the coast road or motorway, and perhaps turn off to visit **Moya**, a neat little town with an impressive church, precariously perched on the edge of a ravine.

Just off the coast road is the **Cenobio de Valerón** (open Wed–Sun 10am–5pm; admission fee). *Cenobio* means convent, and this complex of about 300 caves, hollowed out of the soft, volcanic rock, was believed to have been a place where young women were detained in order to protect their virginity until they married. However, it is now widely accepted that the caves were actually grain stores.

Stop at Gáldar, known as the Ciudad de los Guanartemes, as it was once the Guanche capital. The **Iglesia de Santiago de los Caballeros**, in a shady square, was built on the spot where chief Semidan's palace supposedly stood. The **Cueva Pintada**, the main Guanche site, close to the centre of town, re-opens with an on-site museum in July 2005, after being closed for many years (tel: 928 895 555 for times and details). Now go south towards **Agaete**, the most attractive of the northern towns. It stands on the edge of the **Barranco de Agaete**, a beautiful, fertile valley, usually signposted simply as El Valle. The road goes up to the viewpoint at the village of **Los Berrazales**. Agaete's port, **Puerto de las Nieves,** is a haven of calm among the formidable rocky cliffs that make up this stretch of coast. There's a sweet church, the Ermita de las Nieves, and a new jetty has been built in the harbour, where a number of good fish restaurants line the quay, and ferries depart for Santa Cruz de Tenerife. The road along the west coast winds through barren rocks on one side and sheer cliffs on the other. Keep your eyes on the road until you reach one of the two look-out points, the **Andén Verde** and the **Mirador del Balcón**, both offering superlative views up and down the craggy coastline and across the sea.

Central Sights

The mountainous centre of the island makes for tiring driving, but the wonderful panoramas are ample reward. Pine forests, almond groves, gnarled mountains, sheer cliffs and cloudy mountain tops beckon.

The best and most popular vantage point is the **Cruz de Tejeda**, the sombre stone cross marking the top of a pass, at 1,580m (5,184ft). This is one of the few points inland where you are almost guaranteed to meet fellow tourists. Two restaurants (one, El Refugio, is also a hotel), fruit and souvenir stalls and men offering donkey rides make it a hive of activity. The magnificent panorama includes two rock formations that were once worshipped by the Guanches. One is is the **Roque Bentaiga** (1,412m/4,632ft), the other, the most distinctive, is the statuesque bulk of **Roque Nublo** at 1,803m (5,915ft). It takes little imagination to understand the early inhabitants' fascination with these stark, brooding peaks.

The Cruz de Tejeda is the hub of the island, and there are any number of routes to it, so you could go up one way and down another. From Las Palmas, the most northerly route runs through the peaceful town of **Teror**. The whitewashed houses, many built around graceful patios, have traditional carved balconies. The **Basílica de Nuestra Señora del Pino** (Our Lady of the Pine Tree; open Mon–Fri 9am–noon, 2–6pm, Sat–Sun 9am–6pm) commemorates a vision of the Virgin in the branches of a pine tree, seen by shepherds in 1481. The Virgen del Pino is the most popular saint on the island and a huge festival is held in her honour during the first week of September. Beside the church, the **Museo de Los Patrones de la Virgen del Pino** (open Mon–Thur and Sat 11.30am–7pm, Sun 10.30am–2pm; admission fee) in a beautiful building, set around a courtyard, is furnished in the style of a noble, 17th-century home.

The awe-inspiring peaks.

An alternative route from Las Palmas, through the suburbs of Santa Brígida and Vega de San Mateo passes close to the **Caldera de Bandama**, a green and fertile volcanic crater, almost 1km (½ mile) across and some 200m (655ft) deep. The views from here take in the mountains, the fertile valley and vast stretches of the coastline.

You can also reach the summits via an extremely winding but beautiful route from Moya via **Artenara**, the highest village on the island, where the houses are built into the solid rock. There is a cave church and a cave restaurant, the **Méson La Silla**, entered through a tunnel, where you can get good, substantial, island food.

LANZAROTE

Lanzarote is the fourth-largest island in the Canaries, with an area of 805 sq km (310 sq miles) and a population of 86,000. It is a startling place, representing the triumph of civilisation over a hostile environment; the entire island has been declared a Biosphere Reserve by UNESCO. Its pockmarked, lunar surface, 60km (37 miles) long and 20km (12½ miles) wide, is dotted with more than 300 volcanoes, yet onions, potatoes, tomatoes, melons and grapes all spring in abundance from the black ash. Lanzarote's most unusual farm crop, however, is the cochineal beetle that, when crushed, emits a red dye used as colouring for Campari and lipstick *(see page 19)*. Newer to the tourist scene than either Gran Canaria or Tenerife, Lanzarote has learned from the excesses of its sister islands. Here, small is beautiful and harmony with the environment is the philosophy.

The South

Arrecife, the principal port and latter-day capital, does not have a lot of character although it was given a major face lift in the late 1990s. It has two interesting historical buildings. The first is the 16th-century **Castillo de San Gabriel** (open Tues–Fri

Castillo de San José houses a modern art museum.

10am–1pm, 4–7pm; free) situated close to the centre of town. It houses a small archaeological museum of no great standing, but it is worth the walk across the drawbridge and over the lagoon, on to the little island where the castle was set to deter pirates.

The **Castillo de San José**, a few kilometres to the north, is far more interesting. Built in the 18th century, this well-preserved fortress once guarded the harbour. It now houses the late César Manrique's compact but impressive **Museo de Arte Contemporáneo** (open daily 11am–9pm; admission fee; bar and restaurant 11am–1am). The museum displays works by Picasso and Miró, as well as Manrique himself, and is notable for the contrast between the modern exhibits and the ancient structure that houses them.

The island's major resort is **Puerto del Carmen**, about 10km (16 miles) south of Arrecife. Its long, golden beach stretches for 5km (3 miles) and comfortably accommodates its visitors. The sea is calm and ideal for children. Bars, shops and restaurants of every kind line the Avenida de las Playas, Lanzarote's one outbreak of mass commercialism.

The **old town** just west of the beach has an appealing small harbour area with traditional bars and restaurants and an array of marine adventures, such as glass-bottomed catamaran trips and sport-fishing charters.

Take the next turning left off the main road to reach **Puerto Calero**, which is dominated by a smart modern marina lined with good restaurants and blocks of expensive apartments. Boat and submarine trips are advertised in the marina, including one to Papagayo *(see page 69)*.

The main road west leads through the beautifully tended village of **Yaiza**, with freshly painted houses and a profusion of flowers. Here, Manrique converted a farmhouse into a now-famous restaurant, La Era. Between the villages of

Yaiza, known as Lanzarote's prettiest village, is bright with flowers thoughout the year.

Uga and Yaiza is the entrance to the **Parque Nacional de Timanfaya** (open daily 10am–6pm; admission fee), which encompasses the area known as **Montañas de Fuego** (Mountains of Fire). Just north of Yaiza, at a spot called Echadero de los Camellos (open daily 9am–4pm) you can board a camel for a ride up the volcanic slopes of Timanfaya. This desolate area was formed by a series of eruptions in the 1730s, when the volcano was active for almost six years, and 11 villages were buried forever.

Drive on and turn left at the small roundabout to the Montañas del Fuego. Your introduction to the inner sanctum of the mountains leaves no doubt that at least one of these volcanoes (the one you are standing on) is not dead, just sleeping. Less than 10m (32ft) beneath the surface the temperature reaches 600°C (1,112°F) and at the surface level it can, at certain places, get to 120°C (248°F). A guide demonstrates this by pouring water down a tube into the earth, then retreating before a geyser of hot water erupts. In the nearby **Isolote de Hilario** restaurant, meat is grilled on heat rising directly from the ground – an instant, natural barbecue.

Cars are not allowed any farther into the park and from here coach tours depart to explore the incredible landscape. Any *malpaís* (badlands) that you may have seen up to this point have been a mere appetiser for the main course. The words *lunar* and *alien* are worked to exhaustion in attempts to describe the area and still scarcely do justice to the dramatic scenery. The last period of volcanic activity here began in 1824 and lasted 10 years.

With rainfall so rare and underground water sources extremely limited you may wonder how Lanzarote manages to survive as an agricultural island. The black topsoil is the secret, discovered by the farmers in their adversity. The porous volcanic particles that make up the topsoil are useless in themselves but act as a sponge for the moisture in the night air, obtaining water for the plants and eliminating the need for rain. The topsoil is piled on top of the crops and only needs replacing about once every 20 years.

The most impressive example of this type of farming is the vineyards around the valley of **La Geria**. Each vine is set in its own mini-crater, protected from wind and excess sun by a low, semi-circular wall of lava stones (other crops are also protected in this manner). The horseshoe patterns thus formed stretch way up the mountains and apparently into infinity. There are several *bodegas* in the Geria valley where you can sample the excellent local *malvasía*. You could also visit the **Museo del Vino El Grifo** (open daily 10.30am–6pm; free), just outside San Bartolomé, where there is a library of antique books. Manrique's monument to El Grifo adorns the entrance to the bodega, the oldest in the Canaries, which has been producing wines since the 18th century. There are exhibitions of wine-making tools, and you can stroll through the vineyards and enjoy wine-tasting sessions. Also in San Bartolomé, the **Museo Etnográfico Tanit** (open Mon–Sat 10am–2pm), chronicles Lanzarote's past.

The geographic centre of Lanzarote lies a short distance from San Bartolomé. Here, Manrique designed and erected a stark white sculpture, the **Monumento al Campesino**, dedicated to the peasant workers of the island. The interesting **Casa Museo del Campesino** (open daily 10am–6pm) includes a restaurant that serves typical Canarian dishes.

Rejoin the main road now and go west, past Yaíza, where a right turn leads to the fishing village of **El Golfo**. Here, a placid, emerald-green lagoon lies beneath a cliff that resembles a gigantic, petrified tidal wave just about to break. This is the inner rim of a volcanic cone, half of which has disap-

This bodega is one of several in the La Geria valley where visitors can sample the local wine.

peared beneath the sea. The strata, colours and whirls are fascinating. El Golfo is not apparent from the roadside; you have to park on the rough ledge, just off the main road as you begin the descent into the village (renowned for its fish restaurants) and follow the rough footpath over the cliff. Drive south now to the natural lagoon, **Laguna de Janubio** and the salt flats called **Las Salinas de Janubio**. The coarse salt extracted here was once in great demand to preserve fish caught in Arrecife. The demand is less now, but the flats still provide the salt that local artists dye a variety of colours and pour onto the streets of Arrecife in June to create religious and secular designs for the Corpus Christi festivities.

The newish resort of **Playa Blanca** on the south coast, where the main road ends, is the third major tourist centre on the island. It is also the starting point for the Fuerteventura ferry (a 40-minute trip); there's a marina here, a good, golden beach and a number of hotels, restaurants and other facilities. However, just a few kilometres east are the best sands on the island, three beaches collectively known as the **Playas de Papagayo** – Parrot Beaches. The road is well-surfaced at first, but soon becomes exceedingly rough and rocky. There are few facilities on the beaches, so take a picnic, but you won't need much else, as nude bathing is the norm around here. There are boats that will drop you off there in the morning and return to pick you up in the afternoon, or take you on a round trip from Puerto Calero. They are advertised locally, or you could ask for information at the Arrecife tourist office before heading south.

The North

On an island so dominated by the works and creativity of one man, it is essential to pay a visit to the **Fundación César** **Manrique** (open daily 10am–6pm; admission fee) at

Tahiche, about 12km (7 miles) northwest of Arrecife. Manrique lived here and, as you might expect, it is rather unusual. Built in 1968 over a river of lava formed from the eruptions of the 1730s it takes advantage, at its lowest point, of five volcanic bubbles to create the strange but impressive, minimalist living space.

You could make a detour across the island to La Santa, home of the Club La Santa, a time-share development resort where top-grade athletes come for training and relaxation. It offers its guests first-class facilities for every kind of sport imaginable. The windswept beaches along this stretch of the coast have views of the daunting cliffs of the Famara Massif that lead up to the Mirador del Río and Isla Graciosa. There is not much to do along this coastline except sunbathe and windsurf, but the currents can be dangerous, so take care.

Alternatively, take the main road north from the Monumento to **Teguise**, a fine old town of cobbled streets and gracious mansions that was the island capital until 1852. The 15th-century parish church of **Nuestra Señora de Guadalupe** is the oldest on the island. Across the square the

The Magic of Manrique

César Manrique, born here in 1919, was Lanzarote's greatest artist, designer, landscaper and conservationist. He died in a car crash in 1992 and is sorely missed. There is hardly a visitor attraction that does not bear his signature in some way. In his own words, his works were 'dreams that capture the sublime natural beauty of Lanzarote', and he tried to ensure that tourist developments were in harmony with the island's character. Simplicity was the key — whitewashed walls, natural building materials and ingenious water features are his hallmarks.

The Sunday market in Teguise town centre.

16th-century **Convento de San Francisco** is now a gallery of contemporary art. On Sunday a **handicrafts market** comes to town. Among other things you can buy a *timple* – a small ukulele-like instrument used by folkloric musicians. Several of the old buildings have been converted to craft and antique shops and restaurants. High on top of an extinct volcano, the Montaña de Guanapay, overlooking the town, stands the 16th-century **Castillo Museo de Santa Bárbara**. The views from this wind-blown point alone are worth the trip. The castle now hosts the **Museo Etnográfico del Emigrante Canario** (open Mon–Fri 10am–5pm, Sat–Sun 10am–4pm; admission fee) where sepia photos and nostalgic exhibits tell the sad story of how mass emigration to South America was the only option left for many Canarian families.

You can drop down to the coast now, to **Costa Teguise**, around 10km (6 miles) north of Arrecife. This is a totally

modern resort, comprising several *urbanizaciónes* with time-shares, hotels and apartments designed for a wealthy clientele. Early development was overseen by Manrique; later constructions are less tasteful. There is a handful of good sandy beaches, notably Playa de las Cucharas, where water sports thrive and windsurfing is popular. There is a championship golf course *(see page 83)* and the **Ocean Park Water Park** (open daily 10am–5pm; admission fee) 2km (1 mile) inland.

The road up the east coast passes the town of **Guatiza**, where prickly pears abound and cochineal beetles are still cultivated *(see page 19)*. César Manrique also cultivated the spiny flora into the beautiful **Jardín de Cactus**

Windmill and cactus garden in a typical César Manrique landscape.

(open daily 9am–6pm; admission fee) complete with a working windmill that produces its own *gofio (see page 15)*. There is more Manrique design to admire at the caves of **Jameos del Agua** (open daily 9.30am–7pm; Tues, Fri–Sat also 7pm–2am as a disco or concert venue; admission fee); opened in 1966, this was the first visitor attraction Manrique designed. His landscaping talents have embellished and transformed a grotto and underground lagoon into a short fantasy journey. Ethereal mood music accompanies your descent into the cave, lushly planted with luxuriant foliage. Peer into the black lagoon and you can pick out the very rare, tiny, blind, albino crabs, *Munidopsis polymorpha*, that live here. Resist the temptation to throw coins into the crystal clear lagoon; the corrosion of the metal kills the crabs. Finally you emerge from the cave into a South Seas paradise, complete with a swimming pool and landscaped terraces. A museum here, the **Casa de los Volcanes** (open Mon–Fri 9am–5pm) is a study centre for volcanology.

The **Cueva de los Verdes** (open daily 10am–6pm; admission fee) across the main road, is part of the same system and was blasted through the earth by exploding lava. There is a guided tour that includes some memorable sound and light effects, evoking the menacing volcano most effectively.

At the northern tip of the island is the small fishing port of **Orzola**. This is the embarkation point for a ferry service to the tiny island of **Graciosa**, run by **Líneas Maritimas Romero**. With superb beaches and a complete lack of tourist development, this is the place to get away from it all for the day.

For an unforgettable view of **Isla Graciosa** drive up to the **Mirador del Río** (open daily 10am–6pm), an observation gallery built into the cliffside – yet another of César Manrique's unmissable creations. This is probably the most spectacular *mirador* in the Canaries. Great cliffs curve down to the beach, with Graciosa just across the strip of water called simply El Río (The River), and two smaller islands, Montaña Clara and Alegranza, in the background. Combined with a small section of the northwest coast of Lanzarote, the islands form the **Parque Nacional del Archipiélago Chinijo**. The only sound here is the wind gently whistling through El Río. Besides the huge picture windows in the *mirador*, note more of Manrique's creative sculptures in the bar/restaurant.

If you're travelling with children (or even if you're not) you could visit **Las Pardelas Recreational Nature Park** (open 10am–6pm; admission fee; for guided tours, tel: 928 842 545) near **Guinate** just south of the Mirador del Río (Ctra Orzola–Yé, Km1). In its carefully landscaped gardens you will find numerous species of indigenous plants, while children can visit the farm animals and take donkey rides.

FUERTEVENTURA

Fuerteventura is the second-largest island, at 2,020 sq km (780 sq miles), but it is an arid, windy and sparsely populated one. The population is just 42,000 and, despite a substantial amount of development in recent years, beaches still outnumber hotels. At the last count there were 152 beaches, many of them of fine, golden sand, the best selection in the Canary Islands. Fuerteventura's coastal shelf allows for shallow transparent waters that often acquire a beautiful turquoise colour. The island lies less than 115km (70 miles) off the North African coast, and most of the sand is blown here from the Sahara, giving a new meaning to the term 'desert island'.

Fuerteventura is barren and windswept almost to the point of desolation, but it has a grandeur of its own. Craggy mountain ranges,

A windsurfer enjoys the near-perfect conditions at Corralejo beach.

dry *barrancos* (gullies) and cinder-littered *malpaís* typify the harsh terrain. So sparse is the population that it is said that goats outnumber human inhabitants. However, the land can only support so many goats. Females survive because they are valued for their milk and the famous cheese, *queso majorero*, which is either *blanco* (white) or *rojo* (red) according to the crust. A few lucky males are kept for breeding, but the rest are destined for the table.

The wind whistles with great force in Fuerteventura and may even have given the island its name, a corruption and inversion of *el viento fuerte* (the strong wind). However, the constant trade winds are bringing good fortune to the island: with the growth of tourism the island has become one of the world's leading windsurfing centres.

The North

Most people arrive on the island by inter-island ferry to Puerto del Rosario *(see page 77)* or at the airport just to the south of the capital, but the once sleepy fishing port of **Corralejo** has been transformed into a busy ferry terminal for boats from Lanzarote (it's a 40-minute journey to Playa Blanca). The town has become a bustling resort, and is popular with English visitors. The new developments are not very attractive, but the old harbour area still has colourful fishing boats, some old bars and good fish restaurants line the quay, and there are some atmospheric back streets to explore. There's not a lot of nightlife, but more than there is in other parts of the island.

The beaches, however, are what people come for. There is a reasonable local beach, but just outside town magnificent, long white beaches and dunes stretch for some 10km (6 miles) down the coast. Although these beaches are a playground, the whole area is protected as the **Parque Natural de Las Dunas de Corralejo**, and inland, where nothing but scrubby succulents

Fuerteventura is home to old craft traditions, such as lace-making.

grows, you almost feel you could be in the Sahara. Some 3km (2 miles) across a narrow stretch of water, the tiny **Isla de los Lobos** is part of the natural park. Its beaches are even more secluded than those on the mainland. The fishing here is outstanding. Glass-bottomed ferries depart regularly from Corralejo.

There are two routes south to **Puerto del Rosario**, the capital since 1860, and once named Puerto de Cabras (Goat Port) because it was used mainly for raising these animals. The FV-1 follows the east coast, past the dunes, while the inland route follows the FV-101, where a diversion west will take you to the lace-making town of **Lajares**. At the **Escuela de Artesanía Canaria** (open Mon–Fri 9am–7pm, Sat 9am–1pm; free) you can watch delicate linens being made and embroidered, and there's a large shop where you can buy some of the items.

You could continue west from here to **El Cotillo**, a tiny fishing village with a handful of local bars and some basic restaurants. It is rapidly being developed, and may not remain small and sleepy for long. There are some excellent beaches, great for windsurfing.

Back on the main road you reach the little town of **La Oliva**, with old houses the same sandy-ochre shades as the surrounding landscape. The most interesting of the colonial buildings is the **Casa de los Coroneles** (House of the Colonels), once the home of the 18th-century military governors of the island. Now under renovation, the building has splendid balconies and exudes a melancholy grandeur. Opposite, in complete contrast, the **Centro de Arte Canario Casa Mane** (open Mon–Sat 10am–5pm; admission fee) is bright and modern, exhibiting the works of some of the finest contemporary Canarian artists, including Manrique.

A little further south, just past Tindaya, where the road makes a dog-leg towards Puerto del Rosario, at the foot of the Montaña Quemada, is the **Monumento de Unamuno**. Writer, philosopher and professor at the University of Salamanca, Unamuno (1864–1936) held staunchly republican views that made him unpopular with the regime of General Primo de Rivera. Exiled to Fuerteventura in 1924, he spent six years here, and often described the beauty of the island in his writing. His most famous quote calls it 'an oasis in the desert of civilisation'.

Continue east now to **Puerto del Rosario**, as the capital should not be ignored, even if it has no great architectural merit or sights of outstanding interest. However, the harbour front has recently been landscaped and smartened up, and there are a few nice old buildings scattered around and some unpretentious restaurants where you can find inexpensive local food. It also possesses one interesting museum. In a typical Canarian-style house in Calle Virgen del Rosario is the **Casa Museo Unamuno** (open Mon–Fri 9am–1pm, 5–7pm; admission fee), the house where Unamuno lived during his period of exile, and which is now devoted to his life and work.

About 10km (6 miles) south of Puerto del Rosario, past the airport, is the cosmopolitan development of **Caleta de Fustes**.

Activities here focus around the attractive, horseshoe-shaped beach (where windsurfing is a particularly popular sport) and the well-designed marina. In the marina, there is an area where you can view the fish that frequent its waters and there are a number of boating activities on offer. The circular Castillo de Fustes, from which the resort takes its name, was built in the 18th century, to repel English pirate attacks.

Get back on the central road, the FV-20, and head for **Antigua**. The architcture of this attractive old town, founded by the early conquerors, shows both Moorish and Spanish influences. It is surrounded by old windmills, which have always had a useful role to play on this windy island. One of them, set in pleasant cactus gardens, has been renovated and converted into an art gallery, handicraft centre and restaurant, called **El Molino Centre** (open Tues–Fri and Sun 9.30am–5.30pm; admission fee).

Follow the road south now, passing the **Mirador de Morro Veloso**, with commanding views of the surrounding mountains and the Atlantic shimmering in the distance, and you will come to **Betancuria**, the most attractive and most visited inland town on Fuerteventura, an oasis of greenery on this barren island. Although the river bed here is almost perpetually dry, the town is fortunate in having a high water table. Because of its theoretical invulnerability at the heart of the island, it was made Fuerteventura's first capital in the early 15th century. However, in 1539 the ravaging Berber pirates overcame the difficulties of the mountain terrain (which still makes a difficult drive today), sacked the town and destroyed the original cathedral.

The present early 17th-century **Iglesia de Santa María** (open Mon–Sat 10am–6pm; admission fee for museum) is a splendid building, in an eclectic mixture of styles, with painted choir stalls and a decorated wooden ceiling. Lots of gold and silver treasures are kept in the adjacent Museo de Arte Sacro. Nearby, in a 16th-century farmhouse, the Casa Santa María restaurant serves typical local dishes.

Wander around the town and admire the view from across the bridge, where there is a little restaurant and gift shop. On the main street are two interesting museums (both open Tues–Sat 10am–5pm, Sun 11am–2pm), one concentrating on archaeology, the other on traditional crafts. The graceful ruins of a Franciscan convent, the **Ermita de San Diego de Alcalá**, situated to the north of town, are a place of pilgrimage.

Just south of Betancuria is the neat, pretty village of

The greenery of Betancuria stands in contrast to the rest of arid Fuerteventura.

Pájara. In a shady square stands the church of the **Virgen de la Regla**, which has a splendid carved stone doorway.

The South

The main southern attractions are the great sandy stretches of beach on the **Jandía Peninsula**, running from the village of Matas Blancas at the narrowest part of Fuerteventura, down to Morro Jable. At the northern tip of the Jandía sands are the beautiful beaches of **Costa Calma**, where the first of the *urbanizaciones* is Canadia del Río. There is a great deal of development all along this coast, but some of it is quite well done and there is a low cliff backdrop and a scattering of rocky coves as well as the long stretches of pristine sands.

The **Playa de Sotavento**, some 28km (16 miles) long, is world-famous as a windsurfing centre, with most of the activity focused on the F2 school at the Sol Elite Gorriones Hotel. Here the beach is very wide and flat, protected from the worst of the winds, and, as the tides go out, also very wet. The dunes behind it and a little farther to the south form an idyllic beach backdrop.

Urbanizaciones spread relentlessly all the way down the coast to **Morro Jable**, which is a modern port as well as a resort. Ferries go back and forth to Gran Canaria and Tenerife and catamarans take visitors on shorter trips around the coast. The cliffs behind Morro Jable are covered with hotels and apartments, but the resort itself is attractive and bright with shrubs and flowers. There are numerous restaurants, too, as well as miles of wonderful beaches. The area offers everything anyone could wish for in the way of water sports, from windsurfing (of course) to scuba diving and deep-sea fishing.

There are more fine beaches and coves towards the southern tip of the island, such as Playa de Juan Gómez and Playa de las Pilas, but you will need a four-wheel-drive vehicle to get there. Only the brave (or those who go on jeep safaris, *see page 83*) get as far as **Punta de Jandía**, the windswept southern tip of Fuerteventura and to the wonderfully isolated expanses of sand on the other side of the peninsula – **Playa de Cofete** and **Playa de Barlovento** (Barlovento means windward). Here, only very experienced windsurfers take on the elements. Others just soak up the sun, usually in the nude. It's a long way from the real world – but isn't that what a holiday should be?

WHAT TO DO

SPORTS

In the fabulously mild climate of the Canaries, most sports are available year round. Although water sports dominate, there are some surprises – from Canarian wrestling to parachuting.

Water Sports

Scuba Diving: The many firms offering trips and lessons with PADI-qualified divers include: **Gran Canaria**: **Centro Turístico de Submarinismo Sun Sub**, Playa del Inglés, tel: 928 778 165, <www.sunsub.com>; **Davy Jones Diving**, Playa del Cabrón, tel: 699 721 584, <www.davyjonesdiving.com>. **Tenerife**: **Tenerife Diving Center**, Los Gigantes, tel: 922 731 015, <buceotenerife.com>; **Lanzarote**: **Island Watersports**, Puerto Calero, tel: 928 511 880, <www. divelanzarote.com>; **Fuerteventura**: **Deep Blue Diving**, Caleta de Fuste, tel: 928 163 712, <www.deep-blue-diving.com>.

Surfing: A few beaches have the right conditions for surfing. Playa de Martiánez, Puerto de la Cruz, Tenerife is very popular, as are Playa de las Canteras, Las Palmas, Gran Canaria and La Graciosa, Lanzarote. For more information, contact <www.surfcanarias.com>, or <www.surflanzarote.com>.

Swimming: There are many family beaches where breakwaters have created lagoon-like conditions. Take care elsewhere. Some beaches have lifeguards; many use a flag system: red = don't swim; yellow = swim with caution; green = safe to swim.

Water-Skiing: This is usually available at major watersports resorts *(see Scuba diving for details)*. Jet-skiing is also widely

Scuba-divers on a beach in Lanzarote.

available, and kite surfing is becoming popular at La Graciosa, Lanzarote (<www.surflanzarote.com>).

Windsurfing: The Canaries are a windsurfer's delight. **Fuerteventura** is the mecca. Try the **René Egli Centre**, <www.rene-egli.com>, Sotavento Beach; check also <www.fuerteventura.com/sport>. In **Gran Canaria**, try **F2 Surfcenter Dunkerbeck**, Playa del Águila, tel: 928 762 958/928 762 978.

Fishing: Deep-sea fishing charters for catches including shark, barracuda, marlin, and tuna are available at numerous resorts. For example, in **Tenerife**: Los Gigantes, tel: 922 861 918; **Gran Canaria**: Puerto Rico, tel: 928 753 013; **Lanzarote**: Puerto del Carmen (office), tel: 928 514 322.

Golf: On Tenerife, golf courses include the Amarilla Golf and Country Club, Costa Golf Adeje, Golf Las Américas, Golf del Sur and Centro de Golf Los Palos. The Real Club de Golf de Las Palmas (on the rim of the Bandama volcanic crater and the oldest in Spain), Club de Golf Maspalomas and Salobre Golf Club, between Maspalomas and Puerto de Mogán, are the main clubs on Gran Canaria. The Club de Golf de Costa Teguise is in Teguise, Lanzarote. Most are 18-hole championship standard courses. For more information, visit <www.grancanariagolf.org>.

Off-Road Vehicle Adventures: These are becoming very popular on the Canaries. The many companies organising them include: **Quad Safari**, Karting Club Tenerife Arona, Playa de las Américas, tel: 922 716 400, <www.quadsafari.com>; and **Tamarán Jeep Safari**, Puerto de La Cruz, tel: 922 371 707, and Playa de las Américas, tel: 922 794 757, Tenerife; they also operate in Lanzarote at Puerto del Carmen, tel: 928 512 475 <www.tamaran.com>. **Discovery Jeep Safari**, Playa del Inglés, tel: 928 775 188, <www.discoveryjeepsafari.com>, operates on Gran Canaria; and quad bike safaris are organised by **Free-Motion**, Playa del Inglés, tel: 928 777 479, e-mail info@free-motion.net, also on Gran Canaria. A number of organisations run jeep safaris in Fuerteventura; contact <www.fuerteventura.com/sport> for more information.

Horse Riding: There are reputable stables with instructors at a number of locations across the Canaries. One is **Centro Hípico los Brezos**, tel: 922 567 222, near Puerto de la Cruz, with rides over the Tacoronte Hills. On Gran Canaria, try the school at **Real Club de Golf** at Santa Brígida, tel: 928 351 050; or **El Salobre**, El Tablero, Maspalomas, tel: 928 143 294.

Mountain Biking: Bikes can be hired easily at most of the major resorts, where flyers are handed out in the streets. Free-Motion *(see above)* hires mountain and quad bikes.

Skydiving and Hang-Gliding: **Sky Dive Gran Canaria**, Playa del Inglés, tel: 928 157 325 offers daring visitors the chance to skydive. For hang-gliding courses, try the Parapente Club del Sur, Edificio Esmeralda 39, Callao Salvaje, Tenerife, tel: 922 781 357.

Walking: All the islands except Fuerteventura and Lanzarote are good for serious walkers. Guided walks and special trails are mapped out for Mount Teide, Tenerife (information from the Parque Nacional del Teide visitors' centre), and tourist offices will help with trails in other places; also check <www.ten-info.com/tenerife/senderos1.htm>. In Gran Canara, contact **Grupo Montañero Gran Canaria**, Calle 15 de Noviembre 6, Las Palmas, tel: 928 249 292. In El Hierro, the tourist office in, Valverde, tel: 922 550 302, supplies useful information. For maps for all islands, go to the government bookshop, Librería del Cabildo Insular, Calle Cano 24, Las Palmas, Gran Canaria.

FESTIVALS

The folk music of the Canaries is a reminder that the archipelago has always been a bridge between Spain and the New World and much of the music would be equally at home in South America. The Pueblo Canario in Las Palmas *(see page 54)* is a good place for island song and dance. There are traditional festivals held all over the islands, usually on local saints' days *(see page 91 for a list of festivals)*.

Clowns in colourful costumes on parade at Carnaval time.

Carnaval

For 10 days each year, usually in mid- to late February, because it precedes Lent, *Carnaval* is the time when thousands of Canarios celebrate in style. Shops and businesses close, and young and old flood the streets in fancy dress, dancing to pulsating Latin rhythms. Members of local groups dress according to chosen themes, with magnificent, often outrageous, costumes that can take a whole year to put together. Bands and dancers mingle with elaborate floats. Tourists often don masks and costumes and join in the fun. The music and dancing continue until late, with parties everywhere.

Carnaval is biggest and best in Santa Cruz and Puerto de la Cruz on Tenerife and in Las Palmas on Gran Canaria, where it has all the razzmatazz of Rio's Carnaval and the Mardi Gras of New Orleans. Visitors come from across the globe for these events, and hotels are often full, so book well ahead.

Corpus Christi

After *Carnaval*, this event, in mid-June, is the most spectacular celebration on the islands, although it is of a completely different nature. Coloured volcanic sand, dyed salt or flower petals are painstakingly arranged on paved areas to make up enormous artworks in the form of elaborate abstract patterns or religious pictures, sometimes copied from Old Masters. The most extravagant are to be seen in La Orotava and La Laguna on Tenerife, but Las Palmas on Gran Canaria and many other towns and villages throughout the islands also participate. The pictures are ruined, sometimes in a matter of moments, by the feet of the ensuing processions and certainly by the first rainfall. Only photographs preserve the memory of months of hard work.

Colourful fiestas of song and dance, food and wine, known as *romerías*, follow hard on the heels of Corpus Christi to redress the balance between sobriety and fun.

FOR CHILDREN

With almost guaranteed sunshine, soft sandy beaches, and lots of amusement options on and off the beach, the more popular Canary Islands are perfect for children of all ages. Many hotels have special features for the young, ranging from poolside games and early evening indoor entertainment, to babysitters. Among the other attractions on offer are:

Ride a Camel: Camel parks and rides are popular on the largest islands. Two riders are accommodated at a time, slung on yoked seats on either side of the camel's neck, so it's a great adventure for two children. The most popular ones in Gran Canaria are on the Maspalomas sand dunes (although environmentalists oppose them), and at **Camel Safari Park** (open daily 9am–6pm), Carretera de Fataga, tel: 928 798 680. On Lanzarote, **Echadero de los Camellos**, Montañas del Fuego (open daily 9am–4pm). Also at **Oasis del Valle**, a botanical garden and zoo in La Orotava, Tenerife (tel: 922 322 223).

Go-Carting: The carts never travel too quickly and are so close to the ground that they don't tip over. However, being so low they also give a thrilling sensation of speed, and your only problem will be getting your child off when it's time to go. **Karting Club Tenerife Arona** (10 minutes from Playa de las Américas) has a normal speed track and a fast track as well as various other facilities. In Gran Canaria, **Gran Carting Club**, Tarajalillo, San Agustín (just off the GC-1 motorway), tel: 928 141 238, is popular. **Gran Karting Club**, La Rinconada (2km/1 mile from Lanzarote airport) has a fast 'senior track' as well as the child-friendly one.

Boat and Submarine Trips: There are trips from points across the islands, including whale and dolphin safaris and glass-bottomed boats, which offer a chance to see marine life. In Tenerife, Playa San Juan (between Playa de Américas and Los Gigantes) has *Nostramo,* an original 1918 schooner; Playa de las Américas/Los Cristianos has glass-bottomed boats in Puerto Colón, including the *Tropical Delfín* and *Royal Delfín* (freephone in Tenerife: 900 700 709, <www.tenerifedolphin.com>). The *Golden Trout* submarine operates from Puerto Colón. In Gran Canaria, Submarine Adventures runs a *Yellow Submarine* in Puerto de Mogán (tel: 928 565 108). In Puerto Calero, Lanzarote, *Submarine Safaris* make an hour-long trip; when the sub settles on the seabed, divers feed the fish.

Museums: Children aren't always enthusiastic about museums, but here are a few that may appeal. They will be fascinated by the Guanche skulls and mummies at both the **Museo Canario** in Las Palmas, Gran Canaria *(see page 56)*, and the **Museo de la Naturaleza y el Hombre**, Santa Cruz de Tenerife *(see page 24)*. Near Maspalomas, Gran Canaria also has **Mundo Aborigen** (open daily 9am–6pm), a reconstruction of a Guanche settlement with life-size models. The **Museo de la Ciencia y el Cosmos** in La Laguna, Tenerife is a hands-on place with lots of interest for children; as is the scientific **Museo Elder** in Las Palmas de Gran Canaria.

Animal and Bird Parks: In Gran Canaria, situated close to Playa del Inglés/Maspalomas, is **Palmitos Park** (open daily 9.30am–6pm), with parrot shows, an aquarium, and a butterfly house; and **Cocodrilo Park** (open Sun–Fri 10am–6pm), Los Corralillos, with parrots, monkeys, deer and crocodiles. In Puerto de la Cruz, Tenerife, **Loro Parque** (open daily 9am–6pm), has an aquarium, dolphin and sea lion shows, and a huge collection of parrots. Also in Tenerife, the **Parque Las Águilas** (open 10am–6pm), at Los

Souvenir shop in Santa Cruz.

Cristianos, Arona, has an eagle show, many other birds and animals, and the *Jungle Raid* where kids can work their way through all different kinds of obstacles. Lanzarote has **Las Pardelas Recreational Park** (open 10am–6pm), at Guinate, with farm, domestic animals and donkey rides.

Water and Leisure Parks: In Gran Canaria, **Aquasur** (open daily 10am–6pm) near Playa del Inglés, is the Canaries' biggest; **Aquapark** (open daily 10am–6pm) in Puerto Rico is another winner; and **Holiday World** (open daily 10am–6pm), in Maspalomas, has recently reopened with lots of new attractions. **Aquapark** (open daily 10am–6pm), just outside Playa de Américas, Tenerife is a big one; and **Ocean Park** (open daily 10am–5pm) is Lanzarote's best.

SHOPPING

After Spain became a member of the EU in 1995, the Canary Islands' former duty-free status had to change. The islands still retain important tax privileges, but from the visitor's point of view, although there are savings to be made on watches, jewellery and electronic and optical equipment in Las Palmas duty-free shops, there are few real bargains to be had, apart from spirits and local tobacco.

Best Buys

In Tenerife, local **wines** are a good thing to take home; buy from the Casa del Vino La Baranda at El Sauzal. **Cigars**, hand-rolled from locally grown tobacco, are a good buy in La Palma and Tenerife. Among edible items, *queso de flor*, the famous cheese made in Guía, Gran Canaria, is a good choice. Jars of *mojo* sauce in many varieties and *bienmesabe* (almond dessert) are widely available. Tenerife honey *(miel)* comes in various guises; the best is from Las Cañadas del Teide. Find out about the different kinds in the Casa de Miel by the Casa del Vino in El Sauzal.

Handicraft items *(artesanía)*, including include textiles, baskets and ceramics, can be found in shops and markets all over Gran Canaria, but the best-quality goods are sold in the outlets of the **Federación para la Etnografía y el Desarrollo de la Artesanía Canaria (FEDAC)**. These are situated at Calle Domingo J. Navarro 7, Las Palmas, and in the tourist office in Avenida de España, Playa del Inglés.

In Tenerife, **embroidery** and **lace-making** are traditional crafts, especially patterned tablecloths and cushion covers. Buy from a reputable shop, such as the **Casa de los Balcones** in La Orotava, or one of its branches. Buying these goods will help keep the craft industry alive, but don't expect bargains; if things are cheap, they are probably machine-made and mass produced. **Craft** speciality shops include **Artenerife** beside the port in Puerto de la Cruz and **Artesanas El Sol** in Santa Cruz.

Markets/Mercados: Market are always fun. Prices are flexible and haggling is accepted as part of the process. The biggest, most colourful markets are usually held on Sunday morning. The Sunday morning flea market near the port in Las Palmas is particularly good, and the Mercado de Nuestra Señora de Africa in Santa Cruz de Tenerife is recommended at any time.

Puerto de Mogán, Gran Canaria, has an excellent market by the old port on Friday morning; in Lanzarote, Teguise's Sunday handicaft market is renowned.

Last-Minute Special: A few days before you are due to fly home, order some *strelitzias* – Bird of Paradise flowers – or buy them at the airport. Compared with the price of exotic flora elsewhere, these are real bargains, even when packed in an air-freight box that makes them very easy to transport.

NIGHTLIFE

In the main tourist centres of the Canaries you can find almost any kind of nightlife you want, from extravagant and formal floorshows to cheap and rowdy karaoke bars, plus clubs and music bars of all kinds. In Gran Canaria, Playa del Inglés and Maspalomas are full of them. The commercial centres are the places to go; among the **Kasbah**'s biggest, and most lasting, are **Fantasy Island** and **The Garage**. The **Yumbo Centre** is known for its gay bars and clubs,   although there are numerous straight venues as well. In Las Palmas, the Mesa y López district is usually the best bet for late-night bars. In Tenerife, Playa de las Américas has the most lavish nightlife. **Veronica**'s is the best-known strip, with around 100 bars and clubs that keep going until dawn. Some of the most extravagant shows are out on at **Pirámide de Arona**. **Tropicana** also stages song-and-dance spectaculars. **Castillo San Miguel**, signposted off the *autopista sur* at San Miguel, has medieval nights.

Casinos: There are two casinos on Gran Canaria; one in the **Hotel Santa Catalina** in Las Palmas; the other in **Hotel Meliá Tamarindos** in San Agustín. In Tenerife, there's **Casino Taoro** in Puerto de la Cruz and Casino Playa de las Américas, in the **Hotel Gran Tenerife**, on Playa de las Américas.

Festivals

What with saints' days, religious and public holidays, village feast days, and around 10 days of Carnaval, you would be very unlucky to visit the islands, particularly in the summer, and not catch some festivity or other. Here are a few of the most colourful events:

January: Cabalgata de los Reyes (Procession of the Three Kings): costumes, bands, camel cavalcades. Las Palmas (Gran Canaria); Santa Cruz, Garachico (Tenerife), Valle Gran Rey (La Gomera).

February/March: Carnaval: Las Palmas (Gran Canaria); Santa Cruz (Tenerife) and other towns throughout the islands. Fiesta de Nuestra Señora de la Candelaria: La Oliva (Lanzarote). Carnaval de Nuestra Señora del Rosario: festival of music and dance plus Canarian wrestling, Puerto del Rosario (Lanzarote).

March/April: Semana Santa (Holy Week): solemn pre-Easter processions in many towns and cities throughout the islands.

May: spring festivals, opera festival Santa Cruz (Tenerife). Fiestas de la Cruz: processions, festivities, and fireworks. All places with Cruz (cross) in their name.

June: Fiesta de Corpus Christi: Celebrated in many towns and villages, especially La Laguna and La Orotava, where streets are covered with carpets of coloured sand and flowers. Romería de San Isidro: procession of ox-drawn carts laden with local produce. La Orotava (Tenerife).

July: Romería de San Benito: procession of ox-drawn carts laden with local produce. La Laguna (Tenerife). Fiesta del Mar (Festival of the Sea): water sports, activities and religious ceremonies combined. Santa Cruz, Puerto de la Cruz (Tenerife). Fiesta de San Buenaventura: important local festival featuring Canarian wrestling. Betancuria (Fuerteventura). Fiesta de la Virgen del Carmen: a celebration of Our Lady of Carmen, the patron saint of all seamen. Celebrated in all the islands, in any village or town by the sea; especially colourful in Puerto de

Mogán (Gran Canaria). Romerías de Santiago Apóstol (Festival of St James): pilgrimage, fireworks. Gáldar, San Bartolomé (Gran Canaria); Santa Cruz (Tenerife).

August: Fiesta de Nuestra Señora de las Nieves (Our Lady of the Snows): an interesting mixture of religious piety and general fun and games. Agaete (Gran Canaria); several locations (La Palma). Fiesta de la Asunción (Assumption): re-enactment of the appearance of the Blessed Virgin to the Guanches. Candelaria (Tenerife). Bajada de la Rama (Bringing down the Branches): an ancient ceremony invoking rain. Agaete/Puerto de las Nieves (Gran Canaria).

September: Semana de Colón (Columbus Week): San Sebastián (La Gomera). Romería de la Virgen del Pino: religious and secular festivities celebrating Our Lady of the Pine. Teror (Gran Canaria). Fiestas del Santíssimo Cristo: floats, flowers, and fireworks, processions, sports, classical theatre and poetry readings. La Laguna, Tacaronte (Tenerife). Fiesta de la Virgen de la Peña: island-wide celebrations of the patron saint of Fuerteventura. Pilgrimage to Vega del Río de Palma, near Betancuria (Fuerteventura). Fiesta de la Virgen de los Volcanes: a celebration of a miraculous deliverance from volcanic destruction. Mancha Blanca, Tinajo (Lanzarote).

October: Fiesta de Nuestra Señora de la Luz: flowers, fireworks and a maritime procession. Las Palmas (Gran Canaria).

November: Fiesta del Rancho de Ánimas: revival of ancient folklore. Teror (Gran Canaria).

December: Fiesta de Santa Lucía (Festival of Light): Máguez, near Haria (Lanzarote); Arucas, Gáldar, Santa Lucía (Gran Canaria).

EATING OUT

Travellers who treat local food and drink as an integral part of their holiday enjoyment will rarely be disappointed in the Canaries. There are some excellent Spanish restaurants in the islands, and cosmopolitan cuisine as elaborate or as downbeat as you please also thrives. You can choose to be served in candle-lit luxury or simply go to the nearest fast-food outlet.

If you want to sample real Canarian food look for the word *típico*, which indicates a good value, often country-style restaurant serving fresh local food.

Restaurants

Across Spain and the Canaries, restaurants are officially graded by a 'fork' system. One fork is the lowest grade, five forks is the top. However, these ratings are awarded according to the facilities and the degree of luxury that the restaurant offers, not the quality of the food. Five forks will guarantee a hefty bill but not necessarily the finest food. Some of the best restaurants in the islands have fewer than five forks because their owners give priority to the quality of the food and wine rather than the standard of the furnishings.

A selection of recommended restaurants is enclosed at the end of this guide *(see page 135)*. However, if in doubt, don't forget the universal criterion for sizing up a restaurant. Are local people eating there?

All Spanish restaurants should offer a *menú del día* (daily special). This is normally three courses, including a glass of wine, at a very reasonable set price. If the waiter says '*¿Menú?*,' he means, 'Do you want the *menú del día?*' If you want to see the menu, ask for '*La carta, por favor*'.

In all restaurants the prices on the menu should include taxes and often a service charge (look for the words *servicio incluido*). If service isn't included, leave a tip of around 10 percent. Never eat in a restaurant that does not display prices. Also, remember to calculate in advance how much you will pay when ordering fish priced by the kilo, which it sometimes is.

Meal times are late, as they are on the Spanish mainland; the peak hours are 2–3pm for lunch and around 10pm for dinner. However, restaurants are used to the eating habits of northern Europeans and Americans, and you can get a meal in many places at just about any time of day.

Bars and Cafés

From sunrise to midnight, from the first coffee to the last brandy, the café is a very special institution in daily life in the Canaries. In practice there is little difference between a bar and a café, and you are usually able to get something light to eat in either of them.

Most bars are noisy places. The ubiquitous TV is almost always switched on, a radio or piped music may well be playing simultaneously, and the gaming machines pump out electronic staccato tones as local lads try to hit the jackpot.

Bars and cafés are the meeting places for both islanders and tourists. The price of a cup of coffee buys you a ringside seat for as long as you care to stay; no one will rush you to leave or to buy another drink.

Wines and spirits are served at all hours everywhere in Spain, so don't raise an eyebrow when you see someone knocking back a measure of colourless firewater first thing in the morning. You may also be surprised to see that children frequent bars with impunity. The Spanish consider this quite natural, even late at night.

Tapas are a good way to enjoy the local cuisine and try out unusual tastes and dishes.

Bars and cafés may include a service charge, but an additional small tip is the custom if you have spent any length of time in the establishment. Prices are 10–15 percent lower if you stand or sit at the bar rather than occupy a table.

Tapas

A *tapa* is a small portion of food served in a bar to encourage you to keep drinking instead of heading off to a restaurant for a meal. The word *tapa* means 'lid' and comes from the custom of giving a free bite of food with a drink, the food served on a saucer atop the glass like a lid. Nowadays it is rare to see *tapas* given away, but *tapas* bars are more popular than ever.

Bonafide *tapas* bars, and indeed many simple bars, have a whole counter display of hot and cold snacks that make choosing very easy. Just point to the ones you like. Some of the most common *tapas* are olives, meatballs (*albóndigas*), local cheese (*queso*), wedges of Spanish omelette (*tortilla*), spicy salami-style sausage (*salchichón* or *chorizo*), octopus (*pulpo*), prawns (*gambas*), often with garlic dressing, mushrooms (*champinoñes*), and mountain-cured ham (*jamón serrano*).

Tapas are always accompanied by a basket of fresh bread, which is usually needed to mop up the juices.

A *tapa* is the smallest amount; a *ración* is larger and a *porción* is getting towards a meal in itself. Keep your enthusiasm to try everything on your first day in check. It is quite easy to get carrried away and spend more on *tapas* than on a good restaurant meal.

Breakfast

For Spaniards this is the least significant meal of the day. A coffee with a *tostado* (piece of toast) or a pastry is about the size of it. Down by the port you may well find the fishermen breakfasting on lightly battered *calamares* (squid), which is surprisingly delicious first thing in the morning. If you have a sweet tooth look for a place selling *churros*. These are deep-fried fritters, sugared and then traditionally dunked in coffee or hot chocolate.

Jamón Serrano

A leg of *jamón serrano* is a standard fixture in many Spanish restaurants and in nearly all *tapas* bars. The name means 'mountain ham' and is often abbreviated simply to *serrano*. A *tapa*-sized portion comprises several wafer-thin slices on bread. The ham in use sits on a special holder horizontally behind the bar while others hang vertically from the ceiling. A small cup often hangs below to catch any juices. The hams are cured in the mountains of mainland Spain, the best coming from Huelva in Andalucía. You can gauge from the cost of a few thin slices that each leg represents a sizeable investment. When all the best meat has gone from the bone the leg is used for stewing or soup.

Most hotels offer breakfast buffets, including an array of cereals, juices, dried and fresh fruits, cold meats and cheeses, plus bacon and eggs. Many cafés also cater to tourists by offering a *desayuno completo* of orange juice, bacon, eggs, toast and coffee. In the English resorts it is not difficult to find a full English breakfast at any time of day.

Canarian Cuisine

The local food is usually wholesome, filling and delicious. Unfortunately for those in search of the real thing, it is often much easier to find a 'real British pub' than a *típico* restaurant in the resorts, although much easier inland and in the cities. When you do find one, look for the following:

Rancho canario – a soup of meat, vegetables and chickpeas, sometimes thickened with *gofio (see page 98)*.

Ropa vieja (literally, old clothes) is a mixture of meat, tomatoes and chick-peas.

Puchero – a stew of meat, pumpkin and vegetables.

Potaje – a rich, thick vegetable soup.

All of the above are served as starters but for those with lesser appetites are meals in themselves.

Mojo picón or *mojo rojo* – a red piquant sauce of tomatoes, peppers and paprika. The *picón* version is very spicy.

Mojo verde – a cool green herb sauce made of coriander and parsley. An excellent accompaniment to grilled fish.

Papas viudas (literally, widow potatoes) – roast potatoes with carrots, peas, parsley, olives, green pepper and onions.

Papas arrugadas (literally, wrinkled potatoes) – small potatoes cooked in their skins in salty water. They accompany meat or fish and and are generally served with *mojo picón*.

Sancocho – a stew of salted fish (usually sea bass or salt cod) with sweet potatoes, vegetables and *mojo picón*.

Conejo en salmorejo – rabbit in a herb and garlic sauce.

Surrounded by the Atlantic, the Canarians naturally consider fish a vital part of their diet. You will find most kinds of seafood here, from octopus to swordfish and local varieties such as *vieja* (parrot fish) and *cherne* (a type of grouper). Don't underestimate the humble sardine; they are delicious straight off the barbecue or grill (*a la parilla*).

Meat is just as common on most menus, even though much of it is imported from mainland Spain or South America. Prices are reasonable and the quality is usually good.

Cheeses vary from island to island. The best known is a soft cheese, *queso de flor*, which is made in Guía, Gran Canaria, using a mixture of sheep and cows' milk, curdled with the juice of flowers from the cardoon thistle. This won a World Cheese Award in London in 2002, as did the *queso tierno de Valsequillo*, a mild cheese not unlike mozzarella.

Canarians do not go in for desserts much, but look for *bienmesabe* (literally, tastes good to me), made of honey, almonds and rum. Cakes and pastries are best sampled in a *dulcería*. El Hierro is noted for its *quesadilla*, a fluffy cake made with lemon and cheese, but quite unlike a conventional cheesecake.

Gofio

Made of wheat, barley or a mixture of the two, *gofio* was the staple food of the Guanches and still forms an essential part of the diet today – you even see sacks of *gofio para perros* (gofio for dogs). The cereal is toasted before being ground into flour and then has a multiplicity of uses. It is stirred into soups and into children's milk and used to thicken sauces. It is made into ice cream and mixed with oil, salt and sugar into a kind of bread, not unlike polenta. It is also sometimes blended with fish stock to make a thick soup called *gofio escaldado*.

Almonds, figs, and apricots typify indigenous Canarian cuisine – tastes brought here by the Arab conquerors.

Spanish Cuisine

As the Canaries are Spanish, and many visitors to the islands are from Spain, there are some excellent Spanish restaurants, including some from the Basque country, a region noted for its food. Look for these mainland specialities:

Gazpacho – a chilled soup for which there are numerous recipes, but always with a basis of tomatoes, bread and garlic, and served with various crudités, including peppers, celery and cucumber.

Sopa de ajo – a thick soup of chopped garlic with paprika, breadcrumbs, and eggs.

Huevos a la flamenca – baked eggs, artichoke hearts, beans, peas and tomatoes atop a base of chorizo and ham.

Paella – Spain's most famous dish is named after the large, black, iron pan in which it is cooked. Ingredients vary, but it is basically rice cooked in stock, flavoured and coloured with saffron, plus a mixture of chicken or rabbit, fish, shellfish, sausage, pork and peppers. By tradition, this is a lunchtime meal, but it is usually on offer as an evening meal as well in many restaurants catering to tourists.

Alcoholic Drinks

In Elizabethan times, Canaries wine was served at all the top tables in Europe. Tastes may have changed, but the local wines are still very good. Unfair as it may seem, local wines are dearer than table wines imported from the mainland because they are made on a much smaller scale.

Several of the vines flourish because of the volcanic soil, giving the wine a rich, full flavour. Historically, Canaries wines were of the Malmsey *(malvasía)* variety. These tend to be very sweet, but there are drier varieties that retain the same rich, distinctive bouquet. You are more likely to be offered local wines in country restaurants than in the big resorts.

Rum *(ron)* may conjure up visions of the Caribbean, but it

is also made in the Canaries and is very popular. It is often mixed with Coca-Cola in a *Cuba libre*. A liqueur called *ronmiel* (literally, rum honey) is a speciality of La Gomera. Local distilleries also produce fruit-based liqueurs; particularly banana, but also orange and other tropical flavours. *Sangría* is probably the most popular tourist drink throughout Spain. It is a mixture of red wine, orange and lemon juices, brandy and mineral

The open doorway of a bar in Teguise tempts in passers-by.

water topped with lots of sliced fruit and ice. This innocent-tasting hot-weather concoction can pack quite a punch.

Sherry *(jerez)*, that most famous of Spanish drinks, is not as popular in the Canaries as it is on the mainland, but together with Spanish brandy (colloquially known as *coñac*), Spanish-style champagne *(cava)*, and a whole host of international brand names, it is available in all good bars and served in huge measures.

> In Shakespeares's day *sherry wine* was called *sack* or *sherries sack*. Sack derived from the Spanish word '*sacar*' (to export), while sherries comes from the name of the town *Jerez*, where this wine originated.

Supermarket shelves are full of the same names at eye-poppingly low prices and are always much cheaper than airport duty-free shops.

Canarian beer *(cerveza)* is usually Tropical or Dorada lager. The latter is recommended. Beer is served either draught or in bottles measuring one-third of a litre. Draught measures vary but basically if you want a small beer ask for '*una cerveza pequeña*', or '*una caña*'.

'*Una cerveza grande*' can vary in size, but is often around a pint. Remember that Spanish lager is a bit stronger than some of the lagers popular in the UK and most US beers.

Tea, Coffee and Soft Drinks

The Spanish usually drink coffee *(café)* rather than tea *(té)*. This can be either *solo* (small and black), *con leche* (a large cup made with milk, often in a frothy cappuccino-style), or *cortado* (a small cup with a little milk). Mineral water *(agua mineral)* is either sparkling *(agua con gas)* or still *(agua sin gas)*. Ice-cream parlours sell *granizado*, slushy iced fruit juice in various flavours, and freshly pressed orange juice *(zumo de naranja)*, the latter being surprisingly expensive.

HANDY TRAVEL TIPS

An A–Z Summary of Practical Information

ACCOMMODATION *(Alojamiento)*

Most accommodation in the Canaries is designed for family package holidays and tends to be of a medium-high international standard. Aside from hotels there are apartments and 'aparthotels', where each room has its own kitchen facilities yet retains all the trappings of a hotel. Package holidays tend to provide accommodation in hotel complexes and self-catering apartments, while people travelling independently will find a wide range of options. If you plan to visit during the high seasons (late Nov–Mar and Jul–Aug), book accommodation well in advance through a travel agent or directly with the hotel. For a comprehensive listing of accommodation and rates throughout Spain, consult the Guía Oficial de Hoteles – available from The Spanish National Tourist Office (see TOURIST INFORMATION OFFICES on page 123).

Prices are displayed in reception areas and in rooms. Breakfast is sometimes but not always included; check when you book.

Establishments are graded by a system that allows for many categories of accommodation and variations within each category. A hotel may be rated from one-star to five-stars, and five-star Gran Lujo (GL) which signifies top-of-the-range quality. It's not easy to find cheap accommodation in the major resorts, with the majority of places being at least 3- or 4-star hotels. Also, much accommodation is block-booked by tour operators for the high-season months. The large towns, such as Santa Cruz de Tenerife and Las Palmas de Gran Canaria, will have a selection of lower-rated places.

There is a growing number of *casas rurales* – rural properties or old town houses that have been converted into small hotels or renovated and rented as self-catering accommodation. For information, tel: 928 661 668, fax: 928 661 560; or <www.returcanarias.com>.

Paradors are state-run hotels, often housed in historic buildings outside towns and in rural areas. There are *paradors* in Tenerife, El Hierro, Fuerteventura and La Palma. Advance booking is highly recommended. Contact Paradores de Turismo, Central de Reservas, Requena, 3, 28013 Madrid, tel: 915 166 666; fax: 915 166 657, <www.paradores-spain.com> or <www.parador.es>.

a single/double room	**una habitación sencilla/doble**
with bath and toilet/shower	**con baño/ducha**
What's the rate per night?	**Cuál es el precio por noche?**

AIRPORTS *(Aeropuertos)*
All the islands have commercial airports.

Province of Santa Cruz de Tenerife:
Tenerife: Reina Sofía (Tenerife Sur), tel: 922 635 800; Los Rodeos (Tenerife Norte), tel: 922 635 990; La Palma: tel: 922 426 100; El Hierro: tel: 922 550 878; and La Gomera: tel: 922 873 000.

Province of Las Palmas de Gran Canaria:
Aeropuerto de Gando, Gran Canaria: tel: 928 579 000; Lanzarote: tel: 928 860 500; and Fuerteventura: tel: 928 811 450.

All the airports are served by taxis and the major airports also have regular bus services. There are offices of car-hire companies in the arrivals terminals. Visitors on package holidays will be met at the airport by coaches and tour company representatives.

B

BUDGETING FOR YOUR TRIP
To give you an idea of what to expect, here's a list of some average prices in euros. They can only be approximate, as prices vary from place to place, and inflation in Spain, as elsewhere, creeps up relentlessly. A euro is worth approximately 70 pence and US $1.30 (2005).

Accommodation: Rates for two sharing a double room can range from as low as €30 at a *pensión* or *hostal* to as much as €360–420 at a top-of-the-range 5-star hotel. A pleasant 3-star hotel will cost around €90. Rates drop considerably out of season – May to June and September to October are the least expensive months (and yet extremely pleasant climate-wise).

Attractions: Most museums and gardens charge a small entry fee of around €2–3. A rough guide to prices for some of the major attractions are: Gran Canaria: Palmitos Park (€16); Cocodrilo Park (€10); Aquasur (€15); Tenerife: Loro Parque (€15); Pyramides de Güímar (€10), but most of these are places where you can spend a whole day, and children are often half price.

Car rental: Including comprehensive insurance and tax, rates are around €35 a day from the big international companies; you get a better deal if you book for a week. There are many competing firms in the resorts that will offer lower rates; and cars booked in advance via the Internet may also be considerably cheaper.

Getting there: Air fares vary enormously, with those from the UK to Gran Canaria or Tenerife ranging between £150 and £400 (€210–565). As with hotels, you will get the best deals in May to June and September to October. From the US, flights cost around $980. The cheapest flights are usually available via the Internet, and booked well in advance, or by taking a chance on a last-minute offer.

Meals and drinks: In a bar a continental breakfast (fresh orange juice, coffee and toast or croissant) will cost around €4–5. The cheapest three-course set meal *(menú del día),* including one drink, will be around €8. The average price of a three-course, à-la-carte meal, including house wine, will be about €25 per person. At the top restaurants you may pay nearly twice that.

Petrol: very cheap by UK standards – around €0.65 a litre.

Taxis: Prices are controlled and reasonable. In Gran Canaria, for example, the fare from Gando airport to Las Palmas is around €20. In Tenerife, from Reina Sofia airport to Playa de Las Américas, around €18. Most trips within cities don't cost more than about €4.

Travel Tips

I want to change some pounds/dollars.	**Quiero cambiar libras/dólares.**
Do you accept travellers cheques?	**¿Acepta usted cheques de viajero?**
Can I pay with this credit card?	**¿Puedo pagar con esta tarjeta de crédito?**

C

CAR HIRE (*Coches de alquiler*) (See also DRIVING.)

Normally you must be over 21 to rent a car, and you will need a valid driver's licence that you have held for at least 12 months, your passport, and a major credit card to serve as deposit. There is a large range of cars available, from standard economy models to four-wheel-drive. Automatic cars are available, but not so frequently found, and are usually more expensive.

All the big international companies have offices at the airports and in the major cities and there are numerous local companies. CICAR **(Canary Islands Car)**, tel: 928 822 900, <www.cicar.com>, has been in business for over 30 years and has outlets on each island. Their offices are easily recognisable by the modern, colourful, logo designed by César Manrique. Strawberry Autos (<www.strawberry-autos.com>) also has outlets on the four largest islands. However, if you book on the Internet you will almost certainly get a good deal, and be able to pick the car up at the airport when you arrive.

I'd like to rent a car. for one day/week.	**Quisiera alquilar un coche. por un día/una semana.**
Please include full insurance.	**Haga el favor de incluir el seguro a todo riesgo.**

CLIMATE (*Clima*)

Despite the popular concept that sunshine is guaranteed here, it is impossible to generalise about the islands. It may be pouring with chilly rain on La Gomera or La Palma, while sunbathers bake on Fuerteventura. The mountainous nature of Gran Canaria and the north–south divide of Tenerife means that the weather can be completely different at opposite ends of each island.

There are two rules of thumb: The easterly islands are drier and warmer than the westerly ones (Lanzarote and Fuerteventura are normally a little warmer than Gran Canaria); the sunnier, warmer weather is likely to be found on the south side of an island.

Be prepared for winds: In spring there is a cold and wet gust from the northwest, and in autumn the famous sirocco.

Approximate monthly average temperature:

	J	F	M	A	M	J	J	A	S	O	N	D
°C	17	16	17	18	21	22	23	24	23	22	20	18
°F	64	62	64	64	68	71	74	75	74	70	69	64

CLOTHING

In addition to summer clothes and beachwear, don't forget a sweater or jacket for cooler evenings. For excursions to high altitudes you will also need warmer clothing and some sturdy shoes. During the winter some protection from the rain may well come in handy.

Casual wear is the norm, although in five-star hotels, the best restaurants and casinos, a jacket and tie (although not obligatory) will not be out of place for men.

Topless bathing has become quite common, and is acceptable at most hotel pools. Don't offend local sensibilities by wearing shorts, bikini tops or anything too skimpy or revealing in city streets, or when visiting churches (particularly) and museums.

COMPLAINTS

By law, all hotels and restaurants must have official complaint forms *(hojas de reclamaciones)* and produce them on demand. If you have any serious complaints, the original of this triplicate document should be sent to the Ministry of Tourism; one copy remains with the establishment involved, and one copy is given to you. Try to resolve your problem before going through this procedure, as it will be difficult for you to succeed in any claims once you are off the island. However, the very action of asking for the *hoja* may resolve the problem in itself, as tourism authorities take a serious view of malpractice, and can revoke or suspend licences.

You should also inform the local tourist office, or in serious cases the local police, of any complaints and seek their assistance.

CRIME

The most common crime against tourists in the Canaries is theft from hired cars. If you park overnight in the street in one of the big towns or resorts, as you may have to, there is always a chance that your car will be broken into. Never leave anything of value in your car. Use the safe deposit box in your room for all valuables, including your passport (carry a photocopy with you). Burglaries of holiday apartments do occur, too, so keep doors and windows locked when you are absent and while you are asleep. There is also some opportunistic petty crime – bag snatching, etc – usually in busy places such as markets or at fiestas. But the Canaries do not have a high crime rate, so just take the usual sensible precautions. You must report all thefts to the local police within 24 hours for your own insurance purposes.

I want to report a theft. **Quiero denunciar un robo.**

CUSTOMS *(Aduana)* AND ENTRY FORMALITIES

Most visitors, including citizens of all EU countries, the US, Canada, Ireland, Australia and New Zealand, require only a valid passport to enter Spain and the Canaries. Visitors from South Africa must have a visa. If in doubt, contact the Spanish consulate in your home country before leaving.

Although Spain is in the EU there is still a restriction on duty-free allowances at customs *(aduana)* when returning to the UK from the Canary Islands. This is: 200 cigarettes or 50 cigars or 250g smoking tobacco; 1 litre spirits over 22 percent or 2 litres under 22 percent, and 2 litres of wine.

Currency restrictions: tourists may bring an unlimited amount of euros or foreign currency into the country.

DRIVING

Driving conditions. The rules are the same as in mainland Spain and the rest of the European continent: drive on the right, pass on the left, yield right of way to all vehicles coming from your right. Speed limits are 120km/h (74mph) on motorways, 100km/h (62mph) on dual highways, and 50km/h (31mph) in built-up areas and 20km/h (13mph) in residental areas.

Distance

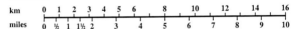

Roads vary from a six-lane highway (in Santa Cruz de Tenerife) and a new motorway system around Las Palmas de Gran Canaria, to primitive tracks in rural areas. In every main city, and even in smaller provincial ones, traffic can be appalling and one-way systems confusing. Do not drive unless you have to in these towns.

There are many narrow mountain roads, where you'll need to use your horn at every bend. At any time you may come across a herd of goats, a donkey and cart, a large pothole, or rocks falling as you round the next bend. Always slow down when passing through villages.

Allow more time than you think a journey will take from simply looking at the map. Driving on mountain roads all day can be very tiring, so take frequent breaks.

Parking. Parking in all the capitals, and the other larger towns is at the least very difficult, and often verges on the near impossible. It is an offence to park a car facing against the traffic, and if your hotel is in a pedestrianised area you may have to park some distance away.

Petrol. Petrol is much cheaper than in the UK and the rest of Europe. Unleaded petrol is called *sin plomo*. Some larger petrol stations are open 24 hours and most accept credit cards. In the mountainous centres of the islands and in rual areas there are very few petrol stations.

Traffic police. Armed civil guards (Guardia Civil) patrol the roads on black motorcycles. In towns the municipal police handle traffic control. If you are fined for a traffic offence, you will have to pay on the spot.

Rules and regulations. Always carry your driving licence with you. It is a good idea to have a photocopy of the important pages of your passport. If you are driving your own car, your own insurance company will provide you with a green card and bail bond, which you need for driving in Spain. If you have a hire car, insurance documents will be provided by the rental firm.

Seat belts are compulsory everywhere. Children under the age of 10 must travel in the rear.

Road signs. Aside from the standard pictographs you may see:

Aparcamiento	Parking
Desviación	Detour
Obras	Road works
Peatones	Pedestrians
Peligro	Danger
Salida de camiones	Truck/lorry exit

Or you may need to say:

¿Se puede aparcar aqui?	Can I park here?
Llénelo, por favor, con super.	Fill the tank please, top grade.
Ha habido un accidente.	There has been an accident.

E

ELECTRICITY (*Corriente eléctrica*)

220 volts is now standard, but older installations of 125 volts can occasionally be found. An adaptor for continental-style two-pin sockets will be needed and American 110V appliances will also need a transformer.

EMBASSIES AND CONSULATES (*Embajadas y consulados*)

Province of Santa Cruz de Tenerife:

UK: Plaza Weyler 8, 1º, Santa Cruz de Tenerife, tel: 922 286 863.
US: Calle Martínez Escobar 3, Oficina 7, Las Palmas de Gran Canaria, tel: 928 271 259.
Ireland: Calle Castillo 8, 4º, tel: 922 245 671.

Province of Las Palmas de Gran Canaria:

UK: Calle Luís Morote 6, Las Palmas, tel: 928 262 508.
US: Calle Martínez Escobar 3, Oficina 7, Las Palmas, tel: 928 271 259.
Ireland: Calle León y Castillo 195, Las Palmas, tel: 928 297 728.
South Africa: Honorary Consulate, Calle Mendizábal s/n, Las Palmas, tel: 928 333 394.

If you run into trouble with the authorities or the police, or lose your passport, contact your consulate for advice.

Where is the American/
British consulate?

**¿Dónde está el consulado
americano/británico?**

EMERGENCIES (*Urgencias*)

The emergency numbers are common to all the Canary Islands.
General emergencies: 112
Police: 091
Local police: 092
Guardia Civil: 062
Ambulance: 061
Fire Brigade: 080

GAY AND LESBIAN TRAVELLERS

Major resorts in the Canary Islands have developed facilities for gay and lesbian travellers, including dedicated hotels. Friends of Dorothy Holidays, tel: 0870 609 9699, <www.friendsofdot.com>, cater to the interests of gay travellers of both sexes; or visit <www gayin-spain.com/canarias>. In Playa del Inglés, Gran Canaria, the Yumbo Centre has lots of gay bars, restaurants and clubs.

GETTING THERE

By air. See also AIRPORTS. There are numerous scheduled and budget airline flights from all UK airports to Tenerife and Gran Canaria. There are some direct flights to Lanzarote, via British Airways, but most Iberia and other flights involve a stop-over in Madrid or Barcelona. Otherwise fly to Gran Canaria or Tenerife and get a connecting flight. The direct flight time is four to four-and-a-half hours. Check the web and advertisements in the travel sections of Sunday papers for good flight-only deals. Many people go to the Canaries on all-in package holidays, which can be the cheapest way to do it. For Iberia, the Spanish national carrier, tel: 0845 850 9000, <www.iberiaairlines.co.uk>; British Airways, tel: 0845 773 3377, <www.britishairways.com>; Spanair, tel: 0870 6070 555, <www.spanair.es>.

For the smaller islands, travel to Las Palmas or Tenerife then take an inter-island flight, run by Binter Airlines, tel: 902 391 392/928 579 433, <www.bintercanarias.es>, or book through any travel agency.

At present there are no direct flights to the islands from the US. Flights go via major European airports; the Spanish state airline Iberia (tel: 1 800 772 4642) goes via Madrid or Barcelona, from where internal flights connect to all the Canary Islands. Flights take 12–13 hours and cost around $980. Connections can also be made via London airports; check with a travel agency, or visit <www.opodo.com>.

By ship: The Trasmediterránea ferry company runs a weekly service from Cádiz to Las Palmas, Santa Cruz de Tenerife and La Palma, which takes around 48 hours. For details, tel: 902 454 645; or visit <www.trasmediterranea.es>.

Trasmediterránea operates jetfoils between Tenerife, Gran Canaria and Fuerteventura, and runs ferries to all the islands except La Gomera and El Hierro (phone number and website as above). The Fred Olsen Shipping Line (tel: 902 100 107/928 495 040/922 628 200, e-mail: reservas@fredolsen.es, <www.fredolsen.es>) runs ferries between Gran Canaria and Tenerife six times a day from Puerto de las Nieves (Agaete) (journey time about 80 minutes; free bus from Las Palmas); and between Tenerife and El Hierro (journey time 2 hours). Naviera Armas (tel: 902 456 500, <www.naviera armas.com>) has services from Gran Canaria to Tenerife, Fuerteventura and Lanzarote, and Tenerife to El Hierro and La Palma.

GUIDES AND TOURS
All the major islands are comprehensively covered by tour operators, whose coaches take tourists everywhere that is worth seeing. They all have local offices but can also be booked through hotels.

HEALTH AND MEDICAL CARE
Anything other than basic emergency treatment can be very expensive, and you should not leave home without adequate insurance, including coverage for an emergency flight home in the event of serious injury or illness.

British and Irish citizens are entitled to free emergency hospital treatment – you should obtain an E111 form from a post office before you leave in order to qualify. You will probably have to pay for the treatment or medicines and claim a refund when you get back home, so keep receipts. Before being treated it is essential to establish that the doctor or service is working within the Spanish health service, otherwise you

Travel Tips

will be charged or sent elsewhere. Make a photocopy of the E111 form to leave with the hospital or doctor.

Farmacias (chemists/drugstores) are usually open during normal shopping hours. After hours, at least one per town, called *farmacia de guardia,* remains open all night and its location is posted in the window of all other *farmacias* and in the local newspapers.

Where's the nearest (all-night) chemist?	**¿Dónde está la farmacia (de guardia) más cercana?**
I need a doctor/dentist.	**Necesito un médico/dentista.**
sunburn/sunstroke	**quemadura del sol/una insolación**
an upset stomach	**molestias de estómago**

HOLIDAYS *(días de fiesta)*

In addition to the public holidays below, many purely local and lesser religious, civic and other holidays are celebrated in various towns of the archipelago *(see also Festivals, pages 91–2).*

1 January	**Año Nuevo**	New Year's Day
6 January	**Epifanía**	Epiphany
19 March	**San José**	St Joseph's Day
1 May	**Día del Trabajo**	Labour Day
30 May	**Día de las Islas Canarias**	Canary Islands Day
25 July	**Santiago Apóstol**	St James's Day
15 August	**Asunción**	Assumption
12 October	**Día de la Hispanidad**	Discovery of America Day (Columbus Day)
1 November	**Todos los Santos**	All Saints' Day
8 December	**Inmaculada Concepción**	Immaculate Conception
25 December	**Navidad**	Christmas Day

Movable dates:

Jueves Santo	Maundy Thursday
Viernes Santo	Good Friday
Lunes de Pascua	Easter Monday (not always observed)
Corpus Christi	Corpus Christi (mid-June)

LANGUAGE *(Idioma, lenguaje)*

The Spanish spoken in the Canary Islands is slightly different from that of the mainland. For instance, islanders don't lisp when they pronounce the letters *c* or *z*. The language of the Canaries is spoken with a slight lilt, reminiscent of parts of Latin America. A number of New World words and expressions are used. The most commonly heard are *guagua* (pronounced *wah-wah*), meaning bus, and *papa* (potato). In tourist areas basic German, English and some French is often spoken, or at least understood.

The *Berlitz Spanish Phrasebook and Dictionary* covers most situations you may encounter in your travels in Spain and the Canaries.

Do you speak English?	**¿Habla usted inglés?**
I don't speak Spanish.	**No hablo español.**

LOST PROPERTY *(Objetos perdidos)*

The first thing to do when you discover you have lost something is obviously to retrace your steps. If you still cannot find the missing item, report the loss to the Municipal Police or the Guardia Civil (see POLICE, *page 118*).

I've lost my wallet/ pocketbook/passport.	**He perdido mi cartera/ bolso/pasaporte.**

MEDIA

Radio and television *(radio; televisión)*. Many hotels have satellite TV with several stations in various languages, including CNN. The larger islands all include some English-language news and tourist information in their programming. TV Canarias is a local station dedicated to the attractions of the islands. English-language radio stations include Radio FM 95.3 MHz - Power FM 91.2 MHz- Waves FM 96.8 MHz.

Newspapers and periodicals. Many British and Continental newspapers are on sale in the major resorts and in Santa Cruz de Tenerife and Las Palmas on the day of publication, as is the European edition of the *New York Herald Tribune*. There are a number of English-language publications with island news and tourist information (mostly free), which cover all the islands but are not very evenly distributed. They include *Holiday Gazette & Tourist Guide* (monthly), *Island Connections* <www.ic-web.com> and <www.news-canarias.net>, and various property-based publications.

There are also good annual restaurant and hotel guides called *¡Qué Bueno!* (separate publications for Tenerife and Gran Canaria), which are in both English and Spanish.

For Spanish speakers, the island newspapers are *Canarias7* and *La Provincia: Diario de Las Palmas*. They have listings of events so can be useful even if your Spanish is very sketchy. *El País* and other Spanish national newspapers are also available.

MONEY MATTERS *(Dinero)*

Currency. The monetary unit in the Canary Islands, as throughout Spain, is now the euro, which is abbreviated to €.

Bank notes are available in denominations of €500, 200, 100, 50, 20, 10 and 5. The Euro is subdivided into 100 cents, and there are coins available for €1 and €2 and for 50, 20, 10, 5, 2 and 1 cents.

Currency exchange. Banks are the best place to exchange currency, but *casas de cambio* exchange foreign currency and stay open outside banking hours, as do many travel agencies and some other businesses displaying a *cambio* sign. All larger hotels will also change guests' money, but the rates they offer will be slightly less than at a bank. Both banks and exchange offices pay slightly less for cash than for travellers cheques. Remember to take your passport with you when you go to change money.

Credit cards. Most international cards are widely recognised, although smaller businesses tend to prefer cash. Visa/Eurocard/MasterCard are most generally accepted. Credit and debit cards are also useful for obtaining cash from ATMs – cash machines – which are to be found in all towns and resorts. They offer the most convenient way of obtaining cash and will usually give you the best exchange rate.

Travellers cheques. Many hotels, larger shops, restaurants and travel agencies cash travellers cheques, and so do banks, where you're likely to get a better rate (you will need your passport). It is safest to cash small amounts at a time, thereby keeping some of your holiday funds in cheques, in the hotel safe.

Banking hours. Usually Monday–Friday 9am–2pm, but closed on national holidays. Some larger banks open on Saturday morning.

Where's the nearest bank/ currency exchange office?	**¿Dónde está el banco más cercano/la oficina de cambio más cercana?**
I want to change some dollars/pounds.	**Quiero cambiar dólares/ Libres esterlinas.**
Do you accept travellers checks?	**¿Acepta usted cheques de viajero?**
Can I pay with this credit card?	**¿Puedo pagar con esta tarjeta de crédito?**

OPENING HOURS *(Horario comercial)*

Shops and offices and other businesses generally observe the after-noon siesta, opening Monday–Saturday 9am–1pm, 4–8pm (some on Saturday morning only), but in tourist areas many places stay open all day, sometimes until quite late in the evening. Banks are usually open Monday–Friday, 9am–2pm, post offices Monday–Saturday 9am–2pm. Opening times for major museums and attractions are given in the Where to Go section of this guide.

POLICE *(Policía)*

There are three police forces in the Canary Islands, as in the rest of Spain. The best known is the green-uniformed *Guardia Civil* (Civil Guard). Each town also has its own *Policía Municipal* (municipal police), whose uniform varies depending on the town and season, but is mostly blue and grey. The third force, the *Cuerpo Nacional de Policía,* a national anti-crime unit, can be recognised by its light brown uniform. All police officers are armed. Spanish police are strict but courteous to foreign visitors.

National police: 091
Local police: 092
Guardia Civil: 062

| Where is the nearest police station? | **¿Dónde está la comisaría más cercana?** |

POST OFFICES *(Correos)*

These are for mail and telegrams, not telephone calls. Stamps *(sellos* or *timbres)* are also sold at any tobacconist's *(estanco/tabacos)* and by most shops selling postcards. Check <www.correos.es> for fur-ther details.

Mailboxes are painted yellow. If one of the slots is marked *extranjero,* it is for letters abroad.

Where is the (nearest) post office?	**¿Dónde está la oficina de correos (más cercana)?**
A stamp for this letter/ postcard, please.	**Por favor, un sello para esta carta/tarjeta.**

PUBLIC TRANSPORT *(Transporte público)*
Inter-island transport

Flights: Most inter-island flights are operated by. **Binter Canarias**, a privatised subsidiary of Iberia, tel: 902 391 392/902 400 500; <www.bintercanarias.es> or book through a travel agency. **Spanair**, tel. 902 131 415; <www.spanair.es>, also has flights.

Ferry services. There are numerous ferry and jetfoil services between the islands operated by three main companies. **Líneas Fred Olsen**, tel: 902 100 107/928 495 040/922 628 200; e-mail: reservas@fredolsen.es; <www.fredolsen.es>; Trasmediterránea, tel: 902 454 645; <www.trasmediterranea.es>; and Naviera Armas tel: 902 456 500; <www.navieraarmas.com>.

Transport within islands

Bus services: There are no train services on the islands, but the bus services, on the whole, are excellent, being regular, fast and cheap.

Province of Santa Cruz de Tenerife:

Tenerife: Buses *(guaguas)* are operated by Transportes Interurbanos de Tenerife, SA (TITSA); tel: 922 531 300 (for 24-hour information in Spanish or English); <www.titsa.com>. The buses, easily identifiable by their green colour, run all over the island with surprising frequency, especially to the resorts in the south of the island A *bono guagua* (pronounced *bono wawa*) is a multi-trip ticket that offers substantial discounts; it can be bought at the bus stations.

La Gomera: Buses are operated by Servicio Regular La Gomera (tel: 922 141 101). There are seven routes; those of most interest are Line 1, from San Sebastián to Valle Gran Rey; Line 2, San Sebastián to Playa de Santiago; and Line 3, San Sebastián to Vallehermoso. All these services run four times a day in both directions.

La Palma: Buses are operated by Transportes Insular, tel: 922 411 924/922 414 441. Routes of interest to visitors are those between Santa Cruz, Los Cancajos and the airport (Line 8); and Santa Cruz and Los Llanos de Aridane (Line 3). The latter runs from coast to coast and passes the Visitors' Centre of the Caldera de Taburiente National Park.

El Hierro: Buses go from Valverde to main centres but are infrequent and should not be relied on for getting around the island.

Province of Las Palmas de Gran Canaria:

Gran Canaria: In Las Palmas, there are two subterranean bus terminals, in Parque San Telmo and adjacent to Parque Santa Catalina. Most long-distance buses leave from the Parque San Telmo station, although an increasing number now commence their journeys at the new Parque Santa Catalina terminal. They are run by the SALCAI UTINSA company, also known as Global, which has a centralised information number: tel: 902 381 110; <www.globalsu.net/es>). Buses to Maspalomas and Playa del Inglés are frequent and direct, and usually leave the bus terminals as soon as they are full.

Tickets on city *guaguas* cost around €1. A *bono guagua*, a 10-journey ticket, is good value and can be bought in terminals and kiosks. Buses run from dawn until about 9.30pm, with a night service on major routes. *Tarjetas Insulares* are good-value multi-trip tickets for trips around the island. Playa del Inglés and Maspalomas services are efficent and run to all the main out-of-town attractions.

Lanzarote: The three lines of most interest to visitors are: Line 1, between Arrecife and Costa Teguise (every 20 minutes); Line 2 between Arrecife and Puerto del Carmen (every 20 minutes); and Line 4 between Arrecife, the airport and and Playa Honda (every 30 minutes). There are buses from Arrecife to Playa Blanca (Line 6), but only about six a day (Lanzarote Bus, tel: 928 811 522).

Fuerteventura: Buses are operated by TIADHE (tel: 928 852 166/ 928 852 162), who have services between the most important towns. Note that for all north–south trips you must change in Puerto del Rosario. Line 1 runs between Puerto del Rosario and Moro Jable (about every 1½ hours); Line 3 between Puerto del Rosario and Caleta de Fuste (every 30 minutes, via the airport); Line 6 between Puerto del Rosario and Corralejo (every 30 minutes).

TAXES *(Impuestos)*

The Impuesto Generalisado Indirecto Canario (IGIC) is levied on all bills at a rate of 5 percent.

TAXIS

The letters SP *(servicio público)* on the front and rear bumpers of a car indicate that it is a taxi. It may also have a green light in the front windshield or a green sign indicating *'libre'* when it is available. Taxis are unmetered in tourist areas. There are fixed prices displayed on a board at the main taxi ranks, giving the fares to the most popular destinations. These are usually reasonable. If in doubt, ask the driver before you set off.

TELEPHONES *(Teléfonos)*

In addition to the telephone office, Telefonica, <www.telefonica.es>, major towns and cities have phone booths everywhere for local and international calls. Instructions in English and area codes for different countries are displayed in the booths. International calls are expensive, so be sure to have a plentiful supply of coins. Some phones accept credit cards and many require a phone card *(tarjeta telefónica)*, available from tobacconists and street kiosks. For international calls, wait for the dial tone, then dial 00, wait for a second tone and dial the country code, area code (minus the initial zero) and number.

Travel Tips

Calling directly from your hotel room is usually prohibitively expensive unless you are using a calling card, or some other similar system, from a local long distance supplier, eg AT&T or MCI. Find out from the supplier the free connection number applicable to the countries you are travelling to before you leave (they are different for each country), as these numbers are not always easily available once there.

A more convenient and economical option, but one that is only readily available in the large cities and resorts, are private companies that have a number of booths *(kioskos)* in stores, malls and other public places. These are usually highly competitive rates and you pay at the completion of the call, so you don't need to worry about having a supply of coins.

The number for the International Operator is 025.

The country code for the UK is 44; US and Canada 1; Australia 61; New Zealand 64; the Republic of Ireland 353 and South Africa 27.

The telephone code for the Province of Santa Cruz de Tenerife, which includes Tenerife, El Hierro, La Gomera and La Palma is 922; for the province of Las Palmas de Gran Canaria, which includes Gran Canaria, Lanzarote and Fuerteventura, the code is 928. However, these codes must always be dialled as part of the number, even when making a local call.

TIME DIFFERENCES

In winter the Canaries maintain Greenwich Mean Time (GMT), which is one hour behind most European countries, including Spain, but the same as the UK. For the rest of the year the islands go on summer time, as does Spain – keeping the one-hour difference.

Winter time chart

Los Angeles	New York	London	**Canaries**	Madrid
4am	am	noon	**noon**	1pm

TIPPING (*Propinas*)

A service charge is often included in restaurant bills, in which case a tip is not expected. If not, then add 10 percent, as you should for taxi drivers and hairdressers. In bars, customers usually leave a few coins, rounding up the bill. A hotel porter will appreciate €1 for carrying heavy bags to your room; tip hotel maids according to your length of stay.

TOILETS (*Servicios, aseos*)

The most commonly used expressions for toilets in the Canaries are *servicios* or *aseos*, though you may also hear or see WC and *retretes*.

Public conveniences are rare, but most hotels, bars and restaurants have toilets. It is considered polite to buy a coffee if you do drop into a bar to use the toilet. Some café owners don't ask questions of casual visitors; other proprietors keep the key behind the bar to make sure their toilets are not used by the general public.

Where are the toilets?　　　　**¿Dónde están los servicios?**

TOURIST INFORMATION OFFICES (*Oficinas de información turística*)

Information on the Canary Islands may be obtained from one of the branches of the Spanish National Tourist Office, as listed below.

Australia: International House, Suite 44, 104 Bathurst Street, PO Box A-675, 2000 Sydney NSW, tel: 02-264 7966.

Canada: 2 Bloor Street West, Suite 3402, Toronto, Ontario M4W 3E2; tel: 416-961 3131; fax: 416-961 1992; e-mail: toronto@tourspain.es.

UK: 79 New Cavendish Street, London, W1W 6XB; tel: 020 7486 8077; fax: 020 7486 8034; brochure line, tel: 08459 400 180; e-mail: infolondres@tourspain.es (no personal callers at office).

US: Water Tower Place, Suite 915 East, 845 N. Michigan Avenue, Chicago, IL 60611; tel: 312-642 1992; fax: 312-642 9817.

8383 Wilshire Boulevard, Suite 960, Beverly Hills, Los Angeles, CA 90211; tel: 213-658 7188; fax: 323-658 1061.

665 Fifth Avenue, New York, NY 10103; tel: 212-265 8822; fax: 212-265 8864, e-mail: oetny@ tourspain.es.

1221 Brickell Avenue, Miami, FL 33131; tel: 305-358 1992; fax: 305-358 8223

For further information check the web site <www.tourspain.es>.

Information on the islands may be obtained from any of the following local offices. The vast majority of them have staff who speak English and German.

Province of Santa Cruz de Tenerife
Tenerife

Santa Cruz de Tenerife: Cabildo Insular, Plaza de España; tel: 922 239 592; fax: 922 239 812; open Monday–Friday 8am–6pm and Saturday 9am–1pm. Can supply information on the whole island as well as on Santa Cruz.

Adeje: Avda Rafael Puig 1 (opposite Playa de Troya); tel/fax: 922 750 633; open Monday–Friday 9am–2.30pm.

Airport (Tenerife Sur Reina Sofia): tel: 922 392 037/922 176 022; open Monday–Friday 9am–9pm, Saturday 9am–1pm.

Playa de Las Americas: Centro Comercial City Centre (opposite Parque Santiago); tel: 922 797 668; fax: 922 757 198; open Monday–Friday 9am–9pm, Saturday 9am–5pm.

Playa de Las Vistas: Paseo Marítimo; tel: 922 787 011; open Monday–Friday 9am–5pm.

El Medano: Plaza de los Principes de España; tel: 922 176 002; open Monday–Friday 9am–2pm, Saturday 9am–1pm.

La Laguna: Plaza del Adelantado; tel: 922 631 194; open Monday–Saturday 8am–8pm.

La Oratova: Calle Carrera del Escultor Estevez 2; tel: 922 323 041; fax: 922 321 142; open Monday–Friday 9am–6pm.

Las Galletas: Avda Marítima; tel: 922 730 133; open Monday–Friday 9am–3.30pm, Saturday 9am–1pm.

Los Cristianos: Centro Cultural, Calle General Franco s/n (opposite Mobil petrol station); tel: 922 757 137; fax: 922 752 492; open Monday–Friday 9am–3.30pm, Saturday 9am–1pm.

Puerto de La Cruz: Plaza de Europa s/n; tel: 922 386 000; fax: 922 384 769; open Monday–Friday 9am–7pm, Saturday 9am–1pm.

Santiago del Teide: Centro Comercial Seguro el Sol, Calle Manuel Ravelo 20, Local 35; tel/fax: 922 860 348; open Monday–Friday 9.30am–3.30pm, Saturday 9.30am–12.30pm.

El Hierro
Valverde: Calle Dr Quintero Magdaleno 4; tel: 922 550 302; fax: 922 552 907; open Monday–Friday 8.30am–2pm, Saturday 9am–1pm.

La Gomera
San Sebastián: Calle Real 4; tel: 922 141 512; fax: 922 140 151; open Monday– Saturday 9am–1pm and 3.30–6pm.

Playa de Santiago: Edificio Las Vistas, Local 8, Avenida Marítima s/n; tel: 922 895 650; fax: 922 895 651; open Monday–Friday 9am–1pm and 4–7pm, Saturday 9am–1pm.

Valle Gran Rey: Calle Lepanto s/n, La Playa; tel/fax: 922 805 458.

La Palma
Santa Cruz de La Palma: Avenida Marítima 3; tel: 922 412 106; fax: 922 420 030; open Monday–Friday 9am–1pm, 5–7pm, Saturday 10.30am–1pm.

Los Llanos de Aridane: Casa Massieu, Plaza San Pedro; tel: 922 401 899; open Monday–Friday 9am–1pm, 5–7pm.

Travel Tips

Province of Las Palmas de Gran Canaria
Gran Canaria:

Las Palmas: Patronato de Turismo, León y Castillo 17; tel: 928 219 600; fax: 928 219 601; open Monday–Friday 9am–2pm; Parque San Telmo, Calle Rafael Cabrera s/n (Estación de Guaguas–Pasillo Comercial); tel: 928 368 335; fax: 928 433 283; open Monday–Friday 9am–2pm, Saturday 9am–1pm; Pueblo Canario (Centro de Iniciativas y Turismo); tel/fax: 928 243 593; open Monday–Friday 9am–2pm and Saturday 9am–1pm

Airport: tel: 928 574 117.

Agüimes: Plaza de San Anton s/n, tel: 928 124 183.

Maspalomas: Avda Tour Operador Tui s/n; tel/fax: 928 769 585; open Monday–Saturday 9am–1pm, 5–7pm; Mirador del Campo de Golf Maspalomas; tel: 928 769 585; open Monday–Saturday 9am–1pm.

Playa del Inglés: Avda de España/corner of Avda EEUU; tel: 928 762 591/928 771 550; fax: 928 767 848; open Monday–Friday 9am–9pm and Saturday 9am–1pm.

Puerto de Mogán/Puerto Rico: Avda de Mogán, Local 329; tel: 928 560 029; fax: 928 561 050; open Monday–Friday 9am–2pm.

Teror: Plaza Nuestra Señora del Pino 6; tel: 928 630 143; open Monday–Friday 9am–2pm.

Lanzarote

Arrecife: Parque José Ramírez Cerdá s/n; tel/fax: 928 811 860; open Monday–Friday 9am–2pm.

Airport: tel: 928 846 073.

Puerto del Carmen: Avda Marítima de las Playas; tel/fax: 928 515 337; open Monday–Friday 10am–2pm and 6–8pm.

Playa Blanca/Yaiza: Estación Marítima de Playa Blanca s/n; tel: 928 517 794; open Monday–Friday 9am–5pm.

Fuerteventura
Puerto del Rosario: Avda de la Constitución 5; tel: 928 530 844;
fax: 928 851 695.
Airport: tel: 928 866 235.
Corralejo: Plaza Grande de Corralejo; tel: 928 866 235.

TRAVELLERS WITH DISABILITIES

There are wheelchair ramps at the major airports and many larger
apartments and hotels make provision for guests with disabilities. The
facilities at Los Cristianos, Tenerife, are renowned among disabled
travellers. For more general information, consult the online magazine
Disability View, Craven Publishing 15–39 Durham Street, Kinning
Park, Glasgow GW1 1BS, tel: 0141 419 0044; fax: 0141 419 0077;
<www.disabilityview.co.uk>.

W

WATER *(Agua)*
Tap water is safe to drink but is not recommended for its taste.
Spaniards almost invariably drink bottled water.

WEBSITES In addition to the websites mentioned elsewhere in this
book, the following are useful sources of information. The individual
islands also have their own official websites.

General sites:
- <www.canary-islands.com>
- <www.canarias.arkus.net>
- <www.canarysearch.net>
- <www.spaintour.com/canarias>
- <www.spain-grancanaria.com>

For information on natural parks and rural tourism:
- <www.ecoturismocanarias.com>
- <www.grancanariarural.com>
- <www.returcanarias.com>

Recommended Hotels

Accommodation in the major resorts is mostly in large, modern hotels. A lot of it is block booked by tour companies but there are usually rooms available for independent travellers, although there is little budget-price accommodation. In the towns you will find smaller hotels with more character and in rural areas there are numerous *casas rurales (see page 103)*. Book well in advance, particularly during the high season. The following is an approximate guide to prices for a double room in high season (hotels are listed alphabetically within islands, not within towns):

€€€€	€180–300
€€€	€120–180
€€	€60–120
€	under €60

Tenerife

Aguere €€ *Calle La Carrera 55, La Laguna, tel: 922 259 490; fax: 922 631 633.* This mansion in the middle of the World Heritage quarter of town was at one time home of the bishop of Tenerife. There are 22 en-suite bedrooms and its facilities only merit one star, hence its wonderful value.

Anaga €€ *Imeldo Serís 19, Santa Cruz, tel: 922 245 090; fax: 922 245 644.* This modern block by the old town is utilitarian, but it's in walking distance of the ferry and pedestrianised shopping streets. Inexpensive, and with great views from the roof.

Arona Gran Hotel €€ *Los Cristianos, tel: 922 750 678; fax: 922 750 243.* On the beach at the end of Los Cristianos harbour, all rooms are modern and with a terrace overlooking the water.

Sports facilities, restaurants, bars, and a wonderful atrium lobby bedecked with green plants. Excellent value.

Atalaya Gran Hotel €€€ *Parque Taoro, Puerto de la Cruz, tel: 922 384 451; fax: 922 387 046.* Traditional family style hotel with stunning views over the town and coast, and in its own huge tropical garden. Some rooms are disabled-accessible. Large heated pool, sporting opportunities and free entry to the Casino.

Gran Tacande €€€ *Calle Walter Paetzman s/n, Playa de las Américas, tel: 922 746 400; fax: 922 746 377.* One of the Dreamplace resorts in various Canarian architectural styles. By the sea with heated salt-water pool. There are also Royal or Imperial suites with their own Jacuzzi, reception and lounges.

Hotel Botánico and Oriental Spa Garden €€€€ *Avda Richard J. Yeoward, 1, Puerto de la Cruz, tel: 922 381 400; fax: 922 381 504.* Set in 2½ hectares (6 acres) of gardens and parklands, this luxury hotel has an elegant and peaceful atmosphere with views over the ocean and Mount Teide. Four restaurants, bars, boutiques and a health centre.

Hotel de Alta Montaña €€ *Carretera San Roque s/n, Vilaflor, tel: 922 709 341.* 'The highest hotel in Spain' is the boast of this new hotel, situated 1,660m (5,450ft) above sea level. Spacious rooms with all facilities including gym and jacuzzi. Activities available through the hotel, include hang-gliding, mountain biking and climbing.

Hotel Rural El Patio €€ *Finca Malpais, El Guincho, Garachico, tel: 922 133 280; fax: 922 830 089.* Just east of Garachico, on a banana plantation in a 16th-century house. Restaurant and heated pool.

La Paloma € *San Juan XXIII, Los Cristianos, tel: 922 790 198.* One of half dozen *pensiones* around the old part of town. The full-blown restaurant downstairs is one of the better places in town if you want to eat at outside tables.

Mare Nostrum Resort €€€€ *Avda de las Américas s/n, Playa de las Américas, tel: 922 757 500; fax: 922 753 226.* Fantasy land in one of five five-star hotels – Sir Anthony, Cleopatra, Julio Cesar and Marco Antonio and Mediterranean Palace (with rooftop nudist zone and pool). Together they provide more than a thousand rooms, 102 of them with their own private pools, with thelassotherapy a speciality. Also has 13 restaurants.

Marquesa €€€ *Quintana 11, Puerto de la Cruz, tel: 922 383 151; fax: 922 386 950.* One of the most beautiful mansions in town; most rooms have balconies. There is a swimming pool and sauna.

Parador de Cañadas del Teide €€€ *La Orotava, tel: 922 386 415; fax: 922 382 352.* In a stunning setting directly under El Teide, close to the cable car. Decorated in Canarian style, and recently renovated, it's the best place to watch the sun rise and to beat the cable-car crowds. Pool, sauna and gymn. Best to opt for half board.

Sheraton Mencey €€€€ *José Navéiras 38, tel: 922 609 900; fax: 922 280 017.* Old-fashioned luxury in the heart of town, close to the parliament, and used by government officials and visiting dignitaries. Tennis courts, casino, swimming pool and a top-notch restaurant.

El Hierro

Hotel Balneario Pozo de la Salud €€€ *Pozo de la Salud s/n, Sabinosa, tel: 922 559 465; fax: 922 559 801.* An elegant spa hotel offering a full range of health and beauty treatments.

Parador El Hierro €€€ *Las Playas, tel: 922 558 036; fax: 922 558 086.* An attractive *parador* in an isolated spot on the beach; totally renovated in recent years.

La Gomera

Jardín Tecina Hotel €€€ *Lomada de Tecina, Playa de Santiago, tel: 922 145 850; fax: 922 145 851.* A stylish complex set in extensive gardens on the cliffs. Friendly attmosphere combined with the peace and beauty of the surroundings makes it a fantastic hideaway. Also an array of restaurants, bars, pools, sports facilities and the hotel's own beach club

Gran Rey €€ *La Puntilla s/n, Valle Gran Rey, tel: 922 805 859, fax: 922 805 651.* Across from the beach and facing the fishing port this is the only hotel of note in this part of La Gomera. Elongated and modern in design, it has a rooftop pool with delightful rooms.

Parador Conde de la Gomera €€€ *San Sebastián de La Gomera, tel: 928 871 100; fax: 928 871 116.* A comfortable, beautifully furnished country manor. It has a superb cliff-top site overlooking San Sebastián and with views to Tenerife

La Palma

La Palma Romántica €€–€€€ *Crta General, Barlovento, tel: 922 186 221; fax: 922 186 400.* Modern building in traditional style with beautiful views. Pleasant rooms, restaurant, bodega, sauna, outdoor and indoor pool and whirlpool.

Parador de la Palma €€€ *El Zumacal, Breña Baja, tel: 922 435 828; fax: 922 435 999.* A new parador on the cliffs overlooking Santa Cruz. Traditional Canarian in style and décor with a delightful central patio, it has pleasant gardens and a pool.

Sol Elite La Palma €€€ *Playa de Puerto Naos, Los Llanos de Aridane, tel: 922 408 000; fax: 922 408 014.* A modern beach-side hotel, and one of the few hotels of any size on the west coast of the island. Restaurants, bars and swimming pools.

Gran Canaria

Buenaventura €€ *Calle Cánigo 6, Playa del Inglés, tel: 928 761 650; fax: 928 768 348.* This is one of the biggest, with 724 apartments, all with balconies. About 10 minutes' walk from centre but there's a free bus to the beach six times a day. Two heated pools and jacuzzis; six restaurants, serving a wide variety of food; entertainment indoors and out; karaoke; gym; table tennis; scuba diving school.

Casa de los Camellos €€, *Calle Progreso 12, Agüimes, tel: 928 785 003; fax: 928 785 053.* An attractive *turismo rural* hotel built around a shady courtyard; 12 en suite rooms, traditionally furnished, in the centre of this small town. There is a good restaurant and bar.

Club de Mar €€ *Urb. Puerto de Mogán, tel: 928 565 066; fax: 928 565 438.* A pretty little hotel right on the quayside, so the comfortably furnished rooms have views over the sea and beach or the port. Friendly atmosphere, lots of personal touches, a small pool and a pleasant restaurant.

Continental €€ *Avenida de Italia 2, Playa del Inglés, tel: 928 760 033, fax: 928 771 484.* Popular choice for families and there's a crèche during the main school holidays. Gardens; pool; massage, sauna and jacuzzi; multi-purpose court for volleyball and basketball; disco; satellite TV.

El Refugio €€ *Cruz de Tejeda s/n, tel: 928 666 513; fax: 928 666 520.* A wonderful place to relax after walking in the Roque Nublo rural park, with a pool and a sauna for tired bones. Just 10 rooms, comfortably furnished and there's a good restaurant, too.

La Hacienda de Buen Suceso €€€ *Carretera Arucas–Bañaderos Km 1, Arucas, tel: 928 622 945; fax: 928 622 942.* Come and be cosseted in this rural hotel set in a banana plantation just outside town. Comfortable sofas on shady balconies, pool, steam room and jacuzzi; pleasant restaurant.

Madrid € *Plazoleta de Cairasco 4, Las Palmas, tel: 928 360 664; fax: 928 382 176.* The Madrid has a long history and bags of atmosphere, which more than compensate for the somewhat old-fashioned facilities. It's popular, so book in advance.

Maspalomas Oasis €€€€ *Plaza de las Palmeras, tel: 928 141 448; fax: 928 141 192.* One of the most luxurious hotels on the island, set in a palm grove just a few metres from the dunes. Beautiful gardens, pools, putting green, tennis, billiard room, gym and sauna.

Meliá Las Palmas €€€ *Calle Gomera 6, Las Palmas, tel: 928 268 050; fax: 928 268 411.* The largest hotel in town, with 316 rooms, right on the beach, has all the extras to be expected from a five-star establishment including a large pool, cocktail bar, restaurants, a disco, business facilities, parking.

Princesa Guayarmina €€ *Los Berrazales, Agaete, tel: 922 898 009; fax: 928 898 525.* Atmospheric old spa hotel is 8km (5 miles) east of town, in the lush Barranco de Agaete. Run by the same family for three decades, it has a big dining room overlooking the valley, a swimming pool and thalassotherapy treatments are available, if pre-booked.

Santa Catalina €€€€ *Parque Doramas, Calle León y Castillo 227, Las Palmas, tel: 928 243 040; fax: 928 242 764.* Set in a lush park and founded in 1890, this is the oldest, grandest and most expensive hotel in the city. Rooms furnished with antiques; excellent restaurant.

Lanzarote

Gran Meliá Salinas €€€€ *Avda Islas Canarias, s/n, Costa Teguise, tel: 928 590 040; fax: 928 590 390.* The island's largest and most luxurious hotel, right on the beach. A stunning double atrium with magnificent greenery and waterfalls inspired, as is the pool, by the artist César Manrique.

Los Fariones €€€ *Roque del Este, Puerto del Carmen, tel: 928 510 175; fax: 928 510 202.* A long-established hotel on a fine beach with landscaped gardens and large pool. Central location and excellent service. Sports centre just 90m (100 yds) away.

Timanfaya Palace €€ *Playa Blanca, Yaiza, tel: 928 517 676; fax: 928 517 035.* A stunning example of Hispanic/Arabic modern architecture; immense lobby with fountains, pools and waterfalls under a huge wooden-beamed ceiling. Restaurants, bars, ballroom, two pools, open-air jacuzzi and nudist area.

Fuerteventura

Parador Fuerteventura €€ *Playa Blanca, Puerto del Rosario, tel: 928 851 150; fax: 928 851 158.* Wonderful location on deserted beach just south of Puerto del Rosario. Renowned *parador* service and facilities.

Riu Palace Tres Islas €€€ *Grandes Playas, Corralejo, tel: 928 535 700; fax: 928 535 858.* On a magnificent beach with a view of Lanzarote. Well-appointed rooms, attractive pool and terrace; nightly entertainment in the piano bar and lounge.

Sol Gorriones Hotel Pájara €€€ *Playa Barca, Pájara, tel: 928 547 025; fax: 928 547 000.* Recently renovated, in an isolated location beside one of the best beaches on the island; an ideal beach getaway. Most rooms have a terrace with sea views.

Recommended Restaurants

This is just a small selection of the many excellent restaurants on the islands. The following categories indicate the approximate price per person for a three-course meal including half a bottle of house wine (restaurants are listed alphabetically within islands, not within towns):

€€€	€35–50
€€	€20–35
€	under €20

Tenerife

Café del Principe €€ *Plaza del Principe del Asturias, Santa Cruz, tel: 922 278 810.* This iron-and-glass art nouveau pavilion in a shady town square is an enjoyable place for *tapas* of such local dishes as *pulpo con mojo*, or for a full meal.

Casa de Miranda €€ *Calle Santo Domingo 13 (Plaza de Europa), Puerto de La Cruz, tel: 922 373 871.* This pretty old Canarian house with wooden beams, floors and staircases dates from 1730. The *bodeguita* on the lower floor has a selection of hams and cheeses. The restaurant upstairs specialises in fish.

Casa Maquila €€ *Callejón de Maquila s/n, La Laguna, tel: 922 257 020.* This is a reliable local with several individual rooms and regulars who chat at the bar. Parrot fish and squid are on the menu, together with simple dishes such as peas and ham.

El Coto del Antonio €€ *Calle General Goded 13, Santa Cruz, tel: 922 272 105.* An intimate *tasca*-like restaurant off the Rambla, serving Canarian and Basque food, such as baby bean salad with lobster and goat in almond sauce.

Canary Islands

El Drago €€€ *Carrer Marqués de Celada 2, Tegueste, tel: 922 543 001.* This prize-winning establishment is run by Carlos Gamonal Jiménez and his sons. They serve some of the best Canarian dishes on Tenerife, much of it their own creation, including watercress soup with yams and red onion, cheese and *gofio*.

El Sol €€€ *Transversal General Franco s/n, Los Cristianos, tel: 922 790 569.* Classic French cuisine is the speciality of the house in this highly recommended restaurant. Open for dinner only, closed Monday–May and during June

Hotel San Roque €€€ *Calle Esteban de Ponte 32, Garachico, tel: 922 133 435.* Eat in a small dining room or at tables around the pool. The cuisine is as eclectic as the ambience with delicacies such as *dorada en sal* (bream baked in rock salt) and *paella duo* (made with vegetables and squid).

Oriental €€€ *Avda Richard J. Yeoward 1, Puerto de la Cruz, tel: 922 381 400.* Within the Hotel Botánico, the speciality is Thai cookery. The ambience here is formal, jacket and tie are obligatory for men, and the cuisine is enticing. Open for dinner every night of the year.

Régulo €€€ *Calle Pérez Zamora 16, Puerto de la Cruz, tel: 922 384 506.* Excellent food served in a typical 18th-century Canarian house with balconies around a patio. Specialities include *lapas a la plancha* (grilled limpets) and *solomillo relleno de camembert* (filet steak filled with camembert). Open for lunch and dinner, closed Sunday and for the month of July.

Restaurante-bar Mirador La Fuente €€ *Bajada a la Plaza, Masca, tel: 922 863 466.* Marvellous mountain views, and a range of local produce on sale, as well as basic Canarian dishes.

Restaurante La Tasca €€€ *Gran Hotel Bahia del Duque, Calle Alcalde Walter Paetzmann s/n, Playa de las Américas, tel: 922 746 900.* Spanish in décor, style and cuisine, with staff in traditional costumes. Some dishes are familiar; some less so.

Restaurante Poseidón €€€ *Grand Hotel Anthelia Park, Calle Londres s/n, Playas del Duque, Playa de las Américas, tel: 922 713 335.* Beautifully presented dishes such as fillets of sole stuffed with tasty small shrimps and spinach.

Sabor Canario €€ *Carrer Carrera 17, La Orotava, tel: 922 322 793.* In a 16th-century townhouse, serving traditional dishes, including rabbit in *solmerejo* sauce, and *gofio*.

El Hierro

Mirador de la Peña €€ *Ctra General del Norte 40, Guarazoca, tel: 922 550 300.* A *mirador* restaurant benefiting from the Manrique treatment. Island specialities are served in a tranquil, modern room with wonderful views. Closed Mon.

La Gomera

El Laurel €€€ *Lomada de Tecina, Playa de Santiago, tel: 922 145 850.* By the beach, reached by a lift. A fantastic location and ambience complement the excellent *haute cuisine*.

Las Rosas €€ *Ctra General, Las Rosas, tel: 922 800 916.* Panoramic views of Tenerife and Mount Teide and typical Gomeran cuisine. When coach parties arrive, demonstrations of *el silbo*, the island's whistling language, are given. Lunch only.

Restaurante Escuela Mirador César Manrique €€€ *Ctra General de Arure, Valle Gran Rey, tel: 922 805 868.* A dramatic position overlooking the mountains at the head of the valley. Worth a stop just for the view. Open Wednesday–Sunday.

La Palma

El Faro € *El Faro, tel: 922 444 051*. In an isolated cove this is a shack with a tin roof, plastic seats and tables and sand floor. What it lacks in style it more than makes up for in the freshest fried fish and endless views over the Atlantic Ocean.

La Gaviota € *Piscinas de la Fajana, Barlovento, tel: tel: 922 444 051. 186 099*. A pleasant restaurant in a great location overlooking the salt-water pools built into the rocks. Views to the north where the cliffs fall into the ocean are spectacular. Good *menú del dia*.

La Placeta €€ *Calle Real 1, Santa Cruz, tel: tel: 922 415 273*. This restaurant, set in an attractive old house, has a delightful atmosphere. The food is home cooked, with an emphasis on fish and meat in a variety of sauces. Closed Sun.

Parador de la Palma €€€ *El Zumacal, Breña Baja, tel: 922 435 828*. Traditional dishes including *conejo en mojo hervido* (rabbit in a *mojo* sauce) are served in an attractive dining room or outside on a terrace.

GRAN CANARIA

Amaiur €€€ *Calle Pérez Galdós 2, Las Palmas, tel: 928 370 717*. Beautifully presented dishes from the Basque country, in a restaurant run for 15 years by a man who knows and loves good food. Small, sweet peppers filled with *bacalao* are among the specialities, and his desserts are renowned.

Amaiur €€€ *Avenida T. Neckermann, Maspalomas, tel: 928 764 414*. Run by the brother of the Las Palmas Amaiur proprietor, with the same attention to quality and detail, albeit a slightly more international menu. *Rape en salsa verde con gambas* (monkfish in green sauce with prawns) is delicious.

El Dedo de Dios €€ *Puerto de las Nieves, tel: 928 898 000.* The best known of the fish restaurants in this little port. Named after the finger of rock behind it, and overlooking the sea, it serves good fresh fish and seafood in a large, busy and efficiently run dining room.

El Herreño €€ *Calle Medizábal 5, Las Palmas, tel: 928 310 513.* Situated close to the Vegueta market, this restaurant is a Las Palmas institution. It serves hearty, simple food from the island of El Hierro, in a relaxed and friendly atmosphere. Large families sit at long tables to enjoy thick seafood stews followed by *gofio* mousse and *bienmesabe*.

La Bodeguilla Juananá €€ *Puerto Deportivo, Puerto de Mogán, tel: 928 565 044.* Tucked just off the quayside, this tiny place is festooned with hams, peppers and fruit. It specialises in Canarian food, including cheeses and wines, plus Iberian charcuterie *(embutidos)*.

La Casa Vieja €€ *Carretera de Fataga 139, Maspalomas, tel: 928 769 010.* Traditional food served in an old country house with rustic decor, but only a short taxi ride from the tourist centres. Barbecued meat and goat stews are among their specialities.

La Marinera €€ *Plaza de la Puntilla, Las Palmas, tel: 928 461 555/928 468 022.* At the end of Playa de las Canteras, this restaurant has a dining room so close to the sea that you could almost catch the fish yourself. Fortunately, they do it for you, and cook it extremely well. Barbecued meats are also on offer.

Mesón La Silla € *Artenara, tel: 928 666 108.* This is the famous cave restaurant, with spectacular views from its sunny terrace, and kitchens cut in the rock. It serves typical, robust meat dishes, many with *mojo* sauce. Closes at sunset.

Canary Islands

Pepe El Breca €€€ *Calle Prudencia Morales 16, Las Palmas, tel: 928 468 791*. The proprietor opened his restaurant in 1962 and has been serving excellent fish and seafood ever since. Try the *ceviche canario* – marinated fish with Herreño cheese. Booking is advisable, as Pepe is a local institution, and the place tends to fill up.

Restaurante Riche € *Jardín del Sol, Avenida de Gran Canaria, Playa del Inglés, tel: 928 769 733*. Easy to miss as it's tucked slightly off the main road, but worth a visit for good quality, inexpensive food..

Tenderete II €€, *Edificio Aloe, Avenida de Tirajana 15, Playa del Inglés, tel: 928 761 460*. On the ground floor of an apartment block, this doesn't look much from outside, but has been consistently good for years. Specialises in island dishes such as *rancho canario*.

Lanzarote

Casa Roja €€ *Calle Varadero s/n, Puerto del Carmen, tel: 928 173 263*. An ochre-building that sits right over the harbour waters. A small bar, delightful dining rooms and a terrace just above the water. Fish and shellfish are the specialities.

Jardín de Cactus €€ *Guatiza, tel: 928 529 397*. Good, simple Canarian lunches are served on a peaceful terrace shaded by an awning overlooking nice gardens. Lunch only

La Era €€€ *Yaiza, tel: 928 830 016*. Outstanding island food in a 300-year-old Canarian country house, with a whitewashed courtyard. There is also an art-filled, wooden-beamed bar that serves snacks and light meals. Yet another César Manrique creation.

La Graciosa €€€ *Avda Islas Canarias s/n, 35509, Costa Teguise, tel: 928 590 040*. The restaurant of the Gran Meliá Salinas is as sumptious as you would expect. Dishes include goose breast with

French beans, breast of chicken with a parfait of liver, sauce of truffles and raisins and some interesting vegetarian dishes.

La Lonja €€ *Calle Varadero s/n, Puerto del Carmen, tel: 928 511 377.* An attractive, modern two-level building with a high, decorated ceiling and marine theme. There's a wonderful *tapas* bar and fresh fish shop on the ground floor and a restaurant offering the very best grilled fish and shellfish on the second. Open every day.

La Ponderosa €€ *Avda de las Playas, Puerto del Carmen, tel: 928 511 773.* The oldest restaurant in Lanzarote (they've now opened a second branch in the Hotel Perla), La Ponderosa serves Spanish and international food in a friendly atmosphere.

Mesón La Jordana €€ *Calle Los Geranios s/n, Costa Teguise, tel: 928 590 328.* Popular, long-established restaurant, two minutes from Lanzarote Bay Hotel, serving local favourites such as rabbit, kid and lamb, as well as international dishes

Restaurante Dominique €€€ *Avda Campoamor, Tahiche, tel: 928 843 096.* Near the Manrique foundation, this award-winning restaurant offers an eating experience not to be missed.

Fuerteventura

Taberna del Pescador €€ *Playa del Matoral, Jandía Playa, tel: 928 876 411. Pescador* means fisherman, and, as its name suggests, this popular beachside restaurant specialises in fish.

Valtarajal €€ *Calle Roberto Roldan s/n, Betancuria, tel: 928 878 007.* A small, pleasantly decorated restaurant that specialises in Canarian stew and *cabrito*, Canarian potatoes and Majorero cheese.

INDEX